I0617171

The Young Preacher's Manual

Caleb R. Edge

The Young Preacher's Manual
by Caleb R. Edge

Copyright © 2025 by Caleb Edge

Printed in the United States of America

ISBN: 979-8-9921579-0-1

All rights reserved solely by the author. The author guarantees all contents are original and do not infringe upon the legal rights of any other person or work. No part of this book may be reproduced in any form without the permission of the author, except for brief quotes in reviews.

For permission requests, write to the author at:

Scripture quotations marked NIV are taken from The Holy Bible, New International Version® (NIV®). Copyright © 1973, 1978, 1984, 2011 by Biblica, Inc.™ Used by permission. All rights reserved worldwide.

Scripture quotations marked KJV are taken from the King James Version.

Scripture quotations marked NKJV are taken from The New King James Version®. Copyright © 1982 by Thomas Nelson. Used by permission. All rights reserved.

Edited by Kalea Ellison | KaleaEllison.com
Publishing services by Antioch Books Publishing
Antiochbookspublishing.com

Table Of Contents

FOREWORD

In the beginning stages of my preaching, I learned much from observation because there were not many books that gave young preachers the "nuts and bolts" of proper presentation, especially for those of us who were green to this thing called preaching. Often, an elder statesman would share a truth of wisdom, but for the most part, you just had to catch what you could get. So when I received the content of this book, I was overjoyed to think that the up-and-coming preacher now has at hand the materials that many of us did not possess at that time. Caleb R. Edge is not only a phenom of a preacher but a prolific thinker and powerful presenter of the Gospel. Let this book become your guide to developing your craft and becoming skillful in effective communication of God's Word. Overseer Caleb R. Edge is called as a voice to this generation. I'm honored to know him and grateful to be a part of his world. Receive him and be blessed.

— Dr. Jevon Goode

ARE YOU READY?

Welcome, young preacher, to a world of endless possibilities! This is where you embark on a transformative journey to becoming a better steward of the call of God upon you.

The apostle Paul wrote in Ephesians 4:1, "…I urge you to live a life worthy of the calling you have received." Paul's plea in his letter to the Ephesian church brings to light the sobering reality that you do not own your call; you have *received* it. Therefore, you are only the manager of a divine calling that God owns. You have been entrusted with a holy mandate that requires excellent stewardship.

But you are not the only one who has been called by God. In prayer and observation, I can see the desire of God to raise a young army that will stand as soldiers who are commissioned to "cry aloud" and "spare not" (*see* Isaiah 58:1 *KJV*)—a remnant of young people who have answered the call as Kingdom ambassadors, committed to spreading the constitution of the Kingdom of God. Gifted young individuals throughout nations near and far are flooding our local churches, communities, and even social media (Facebook, Instagram, TikTok, etc.). Once those gifts are placed in the hands of the Lord, they will be used to turn this world upside down. A group of gifted and anointed young preachers is on the rise!

BUT WAIT! I don't want you to think that the term "young preachers" is limited to people who are young in *age*. It's not uncommon to encounter preachers of all ages who have been called by God but are still relatively new in their experience—those who may say, "I'm not young, but I definitely need to know more about this call to preach and how to execute that call well!"

In this manual, you will learn just that: how to steward God's calling and the complementary gifts that assist you in fulfilling that God-given mandate to preach His Gospel. This manual is for anyone who is ready to embark on this path, has recently started preaching, or needs a tune-up.

Mind you, this manual is not a "get-it-right-away" or "quick-fix" book. Your success will depend on your willingness to embrace a student's posture and mindset and prepare for continuous growth.

So are you ready to become equipped with the tools needed to be effective in your God-given call to preach? Are you ready to receive insights on how to thrive in your gifting? Are you prepared to trade in your desire to be famous for a longing to be impactful? Are you ready to open your mind to the new possibilities of what God has placed within you?

Whether you're young in age or young in experience, if your answer is *yes*, then you're all set! So grab your Bible, grab a pen, and get ready to unleash your preaching potential like never before.

WELCOME TO THE YOUNG PREACHER'S MANUAL!

Chapter 1

Finding Your Voice

S elf-discovery is a humbling journey we all must travel, and it impacts every aspect of our lives. That journey helps us grow and evolve; however, our society has a warped view of what that process looks like, believing that self-discovery hinges on societal expectations, cultural norms, and external pressures. The journey of self-discovery has become less about discovering oneself and more about living up to someone else's expectations.

Unfortunately, when it comes to up-and-coming leaders, the same warped view has made its way into the church. Many young preachers feel they must fit into the mold of what's popular in order to be impactful. Many are convinced that if they want to make a difference, they must sound a certain way, "whoop" a certain way, look a certain way, etc. But why be a carbon copy when God has designed you to be an original?

Don't get me wrong. I know we all have those "favorites" we listen to and consistently watch. We often look up to or even idolize these ministers who become our examples—whether consciously or otherwise. But we must keep in mind that Psalm 139:14 tells us we are fearfully and wonderfully made by God. We each have unique gifts, passions, and styles. God has anointed every one of us with all the specific tools we need to fulfill His mandate. Therefore, self dis-covery has nothing to do with discovering how to fit yourself into a pre-determined mold; rather it is about discovering and embracing the YOU that God created.

First Samuel 17 shows us a great picture of this. To defeat Goliath, King Saul wanted David to wear Saul's armor—armor that David could not fit because it didn't belong to him. David took a courageous step to free himself of Saul's armor of expectation and pressure in order to embrace his own uniqueness, only needing a slingshot and five smooth stones.

When we allow ourselves to be solely guided by culture and

societal expectations, we limit our true potential and become confined to the preferences and performances of others. But here's the truth: Each of us is a masterpiece created by God with unique gifts and a unique voice. As a preacher of the Gospel, you must break free from those limitations and embrace the voice that God has given you.

Ultimately, finding your voice is about discovering and embracing your complete uniqueness. It's about knowing your passions, understanding your strengths, embracing your style and approach, having a clear message, and just being the YOU that God intended you to be. So, as we begin finding our unique voice, remember that it is not about seeking validation from others but about faithfully stewarding the gifts and passions placed within us. Let's work!

Explore Your Unique Gifts

Because God has called you into this preaching vocation, He has equipped you with the gifts needed to accompany your call. You are a multi-gifted individual who is called to preach and serve, and every gift you possess is a tool designed to make you effective in your God-given assignment. In Romans 12:6 and 7, the apostle Paul provided more insight into this process of self-discovery and the uniqueness of the gifts given to each member of the Body of Christ:

> **We have different gifts, according to the grace given to each of us. If your gift is prophesying, then prophesy in accordance with your faith; if it is serving, then serve; if it is teaching, then teach.**

There are two necessary pieces of this passage that I need to point out before we continue: *grace* and *faith*.

We have all been given gifts, but the reason they can be utilized is due to the *grace* of God. You may have heard or learned that the meaning of "grace" is *unmerited favor*. That is one biblical definition of the word. But another biblically accurate and applicable definition of "grace" is *divine enablement and empowerment*. In other words, God favors us with His supernatural help so that we can use our gifts effectively. Our gifts vary from person to person, and those gifts are only operational due to heavenly assistance that goes beyond our natural strength. This serves as a reminder that our gifts are not meant to be used for personal gain or pride. Every gift of God is *graced* to us for the benefit and service of others. But let's dive deeper into this.

For a gift to be effective, you must be graced for it. It means that God's presence on the gift is essential in using that gift meaningfully. Simply put, for any gift to truly have an impact, it must be accompanied by God's presence. Being gifted in ministry is not only about possessing the gift itself; rather, it is about relying on the empowerment of God to enable us to operate in it with wisdom, effectiveness, and love. Absent of the grace of God, your gift is merely a talent or ability that lacks the supernatural power to transform lives for the glory of God.

You may ask, "How do I determine the difference between a graced gift and a mere talent or ability?" The answer is simple, but I'll present it as a question so that you can arrive at your own answer: What abilities do you have that require a dependence on God in order for them to flow and be effective? What does God give you the ability to do that results in the transformed lives of those who encounter it? When you find that answer, that is what you're graced to do. But this is where the second necessary component of Romans 12:6 and 7 comes into play—*faith*!

Faith is the lens through which we must view our gifts. Faith structures our perspective and mindset when it comes to using our gifts. Just as a lens helps us see things clearly, faith helps us clearly see God's plans for our gifts and helps us step out boldly, knowing that God will use our gifts to bring Him glory.

Keep in mind that your faith should not be in the gift itself. Your faith should be in God who has graced that gift. Without faith in God's divine empowerment, your gifts will forever be prisoners of your limitations. To break beyond the limitations of your strength, you must have confidence in God's power and rely on His strength to use your gift in a way that will glorify Him and bless those who encounter you.

Whether someone operates in the gift of teaching, exhortation, leadership, empathy or encouragement, or a more practical gift like communication, singing, organization, or technology, having faith in the grace that God has placed on the gift in your life can transform a mere talent or ability into an effective weapon in the arsenal of the young preacher. This weapon can be a powerful tool for destroying the bondage so many people are trapped in, but it only works by the grace of God and your faith in that grace. This discovery is the "bread and butter" of an influential young preacher.

You must remember that God's heart is always toward people; everything He does is to reach people and change lives. God never gifts you to become a solo act with the sole purpose of showing off your skills; He calls you to use those abilities to impact the lives of others for His glory. You are gifted *for a purpose.*

But because we are all human, there are often obstacles we must overcome in order to successfully navigate our gifts. Often we can find ourselves getting in our own way because of a destructive or unhealthy mindset. Allow me to caution you of the challenges you may face in discovering and operating in your gift. I have observed two common blockades that, if left unaddressed, will halt and pro-long your journey of finding your voice.

Reject Self-Doubt

In my time in ministry, I've seen many young preachers deal with the fear of rejection from people, imposter syndrome (feeling like they don't deserve to be in their role), perfectionism, lack of confidence, and so much more. All of these are manifestations of self-doubt.

Self-doubt will have you seated in the driver's seat of a fully gassed car, ready to ride, but with your foot on the brake pedal. Self-doubt will never allow you to fully embrace who you uniquely are and the voice God has given you; you'll be too busy second-guessing everything you do.

We discussed earlier how faith is essential to discovering and operating in your gift. Faith allows you to boldly step out and share your gift and message with the world. Self-doubt counteracts that by placing you in constant hesitation and uncertainty, limiting the impact you're destined to make. Remember: self-doubt is a common part of the human experience, but it's only a feeling. Don't ever see it as a reflection of your worth or potential.

When you recognize self-doubt creeping into your thoughts and actions, you must make a conscious effort not to believe the lies that the doubts present to your mind. Negative thoughts will always come, but you are not to be led by them. Instead of letting those negative thoughts dictate what you do, you should mentally distance yourself from them by replacing those thoughts with the truth of God's Word.

When thoughts of self-doubt begin to enter your mind, speaking the Word of God will reinforce your belief in the truth about yourself over the lie. When you elevate God's Word above everything else and allow it to govern you, self-doubt won't be able to control your actions or decisions, allowing you to move forward with confidence and faith in God's grace on your abilities and the unique voice God has given you.

In your own strength, you would never be able to accomplish all that God has set before you. But He has not asked you to do this in your own strength! Put your trust in God. After all, He is the one who called you; you didn't call yourself. He would not call you to do something without equipping you to carry it out.

Even in the function of your assignment, God is with you (*see* Joshua 1:9). Putting faith in God's empowerment and guidance gives you strength and courage to know that you will never be alone in the face of self-doubt. God Himself is with you every step of the way.

Avoid Comparison

At the beginning of the chapter, we discussed societal pressures and expectations. One road to succumbing to those pressures is the road of comparison. Comparison will cause you to make others your measuring stick of success and effectiveness rather than embracing your voice and your unique calling.

Anytime you feel inadequate or pressured to imitate someone else's style, comparison is likely at work. The major damage of comparison is that it negatively redirects your focus. Instead of focusing on lives transforming and the glory of God being revealed, you will focus on conforming to societal expectations.

The apostle Paul said that when we compare ourselves to others, we are not wise (*see* 2 Corinthians 10:12). Anytime we compare our progression, gift function, and ministry to others, it's proof that we do not value our own unique measure of grace, which is a dishonor to God. He has created each of us with very specific plans in mind, and to dismiss or minimize His call is truly a tragedy.

Young preacher, you must never forget to embrace the individuality God has blessed you with rather than imitate someone else. Imitating someone else only results in a cheap rendition of a call that belongs to another person—it will never fit you quite right. There is a call that was designed specifically for you, and your job is to discover and embrace it as your own. There's only one you in the world, and if you're too busy trying to compare yourself to someone else, who will be the genuine and authentic you?

God has you in the right place at the right time. Keep your eyes on the road God has set for you; you will arrive at the place God wants you to be when He wants you there. We may be driving different speeds from one another, but we're all working toward hearing the same thing: "Well done, my good and faithful servant" (Matthew 25:21).

Stir Up the Gift

Ultimately, it is His will and pleasure we are seeking. But once we've found and embraced God's call on our life, there is more work to be done. Exploring your unique gifts is just the beginning. According to Second Timothy 1:6, you must "stir up" your gifts.

But what does it mean to stir up your gift? Have you ever cooked anything on a barbecue grill? Any grill master knows that if the coals start to get dull or lose their heat, all you have to do is stir them up, and the fire will reignite. In the same way, the gifts that God gives us must be actively cultivated and developed, but they must also be stirred.

Young preacher, never allow those gifts God has graced you to possess to lie dormant or become overshadowed by self-doubt and comparison. When you intentionally nurture your gifts, you'll embark upon a journey of everlasting effectiveness.

Wait! You may be wondering, "How do I stir my gifts?" Well,

I'm glad you asked! Here are some surefire ways to keep your gifts stirred and on fire:

- Study and immerse yourself in the Word of God.
- Seek and utilize mentorship.
- Practice (yes, I did say *practice*)!
- Attend trusted and verified workshops, conferences, seminars, etc.
- Remain teachable and embrace correction.

I encourage you to hold fast to these truths as you progress through your journey to find your voice. We have much more work to do to stir the uniqueness within you. Let's continue!

Discover Your Passions

In discussing this portion of the subject matter, I want to approach the topic of passion from a vantage point you may not have previously considered. Let's talk about anger.

Within you are things that God has given you righteous anger toward. You might have heard this referred to as a "burden." In your spirit, there is a righteous anger toward a need in the world, in your community, or even in your family that is not being met.

Whether our heart goes out to women who are seeking guidance, youth in need of a righteous role model, or a community longing for an activist, we all feel burdened for *something* when we see certain needs remaining unmet.

But along with the burden within you, there is also a solution that God has designed you to carry out. You were created with a specific purpose; you are the miraculous answer to a problem in the world that God is endeavoring to solve. And God's solutions can manifest in many ways: through music, ministry, business endeavors, and so much more.

For example, this manual you hold in your hands was written with righteous anger—a burden. I was frustrated with seeing so many young preachers imitating others and ministering without depth. I was righteously angry at the number of young preachers who were just seeking popularity and platforms for showmanship with nothing but "whooping" and "praise breaks." Therefore, that burden became my passion.

Please note: God gave us all emotions, including permission to be angry (*See* Ephesians 4:26). If we acknowledge that our emotions come from God, then returning those emotions to Him can glorify Him.

When we submit our emotions to God and allow Him to use them to help us understand His heart, He can point us in the direction of a need He wants to meet. Rather than allowing our emotions to drive us and dictate our actions, we should submit them to God, which produces results *and* glorifies Him!

This is what Psalm 37:4 (*NKJV*) means when it says, "Delight yourself also in the Lord, and He shall give you the desires of your heart." Our typical understanding of this verse is that God will give us what we want. Although God surely can give us what we want, there may be something else to learn from this verse.

Allow me to invite you in on another perspective: When we delight ourselves in God's will and decisions, He imparts to our heart His passions. God wants to show our heart what to want, even if it doesn't align with what we want for ourself. Read that again.

When we intentionally delight ourselves in the Lord, He plants passions and burdens within us that align us with His will, not just our desires. He guides us toward fulfilling His purpose for our lives as He uses the unique gifts and passions He has given us. God needs a young preacher who is willing to partner with Him in fulfilling His will on the earth.

As a matter of fact, your sonship to God is proven in how willing you are to do the will of the Father. Jesus exemplified that when He said to His disciples, "For I have come down from heaven, not to do my own will but the will of him who sent Me" (John 6:38 *NKJV*). Our identity as children of God is demonstrated by how willing we are to align ourselves with and carry out the will of God.

The world needs young preachers filled with God's passions and burdens who will fulfill just that, not their own agenda. But as we learned in Psalm 37:4, we discover those passions by delighting in the Lord. That's where it all starts.

Here are a few practical ways to develop a lifestyle of delighting in the Lord:

11

- Spend time in prayer.
- Study and meditate on God's Word.
- Worship.
- Serve others.
- Live in obedience to God's Word.

This is how you discover your passions. Through this journey of drawing closer to and aligning with God, you'll uncover the unique passions and burdens He has placed within you for His divine use.

Understand Your Style

Now let's look into who you are as a preacher and how your style can impact your message. The goal is for you to discover how your graced gifts, passions, personality, and anointing all intertwine to create a powerful impact on a congregation by the glory of God. He is masterful in His creativity; when He designed you and laid out the plan for your life, He carefully thought out every detail and how every part would work together. Every part of you—spirit, soul, and body—was taken into consideration when He planned your life, and there is no one on this earth who can fulfill your call—*except you.*

When God anoints you to a preaching call, He pours His power into every aspect of who you are, including your unique personality. It's pretty incredible because you don't have to change who you are at your core for God to use you. After all, He is the One who created you in the first place, right? When your personality is surrendered to God, it becomes a unique, one-of-a-kind vessel for His glory to shine through.

Unfortunately, time after time, I've seen young preachers seemingly "transform" into an old man—deepening their voices, talking with a slower cadence, gaining a sudden limp in their walk—all to seem more mature than they are. They haven't realized that God has already placed His power on the essence of who they are, and they are missing out on a unique expression of God's power through them.

Consider Saul, who later became the apostle Paul, as an example (*see* Acts 9). Saul was a tenacious person who was quite witty. Everything changed when he encountered Jesus on the road to

Damascus, but his tenacious and witty core was redirected toward spreading the Gospel.

Paul's personality traits were always meant to bring God glory; he had merely been using them the wrong way. So when he encountered the presence of God and the person of Jesus, not only was he redeemed from his old lifestyle, but his personality was restored and reset to its original intended use.

I want to encourage you to become comfortable with the YOU God made. When you do, you'll unlock the YOU God wants to anoint. But even beyond that, your style must be developed and understood.

The key to finding your voice is tapping into your unique preaching potential. By doing so, you can avoid falling into the trap of a mediocre ministry, where you imitate what you've seen others do. Instead, the goal is to uncover who you truly are as a preacher and understand your style so that it can be developed for impact.

Be Authentic

As we learned earlier, being yourself is incredibly important, especially when it comes to preaching. Many young preachers struggle with the pressure to imitate popular preachers or conform to certain cultural and societal expectations. This will limit their potential and prevent them from fully embracing their voice and style. But once they embrace their authenticity, they'll experience a new-found sense of freedom and confidence.

This freedom arises from being true to yourself and embracing God's specific purpose for you. Therefore, if freedom is one of the results of authenticity, then the opposite also holds true: Bondage results from imitation and being a false version of who you are. Imitation restricts your individuality.

When you imitate others, you can become trapped by those expectations and lose sight of who God has called you to be as a preacher. The apostle Paul instructed us not to conform to this world's mindsets, expectations, or limitations but to be transformed by the renewing of our mind (*see* Romans 12:2). When we heed the apostle's directions, we will arrive at the place of authenticity. That's where freedom starts. But there's another level to this that I want to explore with you.

Freedom is the gateway to genuine confidence. It's a confidence that recognizes God's grace in your life and empowers you to express your authentic self fully. Remember that our confidence as preachers doesn't come from our abilities or talents. Instead, it comes from our unwavering trust and confidence in God, who promised never to leave nor forsake us (*see* Hebrews 13:5). Second Corinthians 4:7 says that we are like jars of clay, and that the true power comes from God, not ourselves. So our confidence is not in our treasure but in the God who entrusted it to us.

When you're authentically who God has called you to be, people can sense your genuineness, and it builds trust. This trust is built when you show that you are true to yourself and your message. People need to see that you are not just putting on a show or trying to be someone you're not. When you allow your true self to shine through, it creates a connection with people and fosters trust between you and the congregation and between you and God.

We'll discuss this in further detail in a later chapter!

Understand Your Audience

Imagine stepping into the pulpit, ready to preach to a congregation. You've spent hours upon hours preparing and crafting your sermon with great information and profound revelation but never took the time to consider who you would be preaching to. By neglecting to consider your audience, you missed a prime opportunity to establish a genuine connection and make a lasting impact on the people God entrusted to your care.

In First Corinthians 9:22, Paul said, "...I have become all things to all people so that by all possible means I might save some." Paul was able to adapt his approach without compromising his authenticity or the core message of the Gospel. He intentionally connected with audiences to ensure that the message resonated with each individual in a meaningful way.

For example, years ago I preached for a youth conference in Nassau, Bahamas. I referred to American football to help clarify a point I had presented during the sermon. I made the mistake of assuming that just because football was prevalent in my culture, it was commonplace in every culture. By examining the faces of the congregation, I could tell that my point was still unclear. I failed to understand my audience.

The next night, I changed my approach. After researching, I found that in the Bahamas, the primary sport is soccer rather than American football. When I used a soccer reference instead, a near-instant connection between the congregation and me paved the way for a more significant impact.

As you can see, having a powerful sermon is only *part* of the equation. It would help if you strived to establish a genuine connection with the audience to ensure they truly understand and engage with your message. Without that connection, even the most well-crafted sermon will fall flat. Connecting with your audience builds a bridge of understanding for your message to resonate in the hearts of your listeners.

Understanding your audience is about knowing their needs, backgrounds, and perspectives based on their cultural, social, and spiritual context. Additionally, understanding your audience's age range and educational background is critical to being relatable to your listeners. This awareness will help your message connect with the audience more personally. It's all about meeting them where they are and speaking in a way that resonates with their experiences and knowledge.

Here's a list of a few suggested questions you can ask to get a better understanding of the audience you are ministering to:

- What is the demographic makeup (age, gender, cultural background, etc.) of my audience?
- What are the spiritual needs and challenges of my audience?
- What is my audience seeking from a sermon?
- What are the values and beliefs of my audience?
- What are some cultural or societal factors that may influence the perspectives of my audience?
- What are the expectations of my audience for the length and structure of a sermon?
- What are the spiritual backgrounds or denominational affiliations of my audience?

As a preacher, you can explore many other questions to truly understand the audience you're ministering to. These inquiries will provide valuable insights and knowledge about those you are called to serve, and you will make a greater impact with your delivery.

Exploring Preaching Styles

Before we discuss this topic, let's establish a foundational truth. It's crucial to prioritize the intentional development of your study and message before you focus on refining your style. Our culture has focused so much on showmanship in ministry, such as fiery catchphrases and "whooping," that it has shaped a generation of preachers who feel compelled to perform in that same manner in order to be heard.

Think of your style as the "icing on the cake." However, the development of your study and your message truly give your ministry the substance it needs. Each preacher possesses a distinctive style, whether he or she has discovered it or not. Your style is part of honing your individuality in your preaching journey. When you find it, you will connect with your audience more authentically and effectively. Your style will cause you to stand out and make a lasting impact on the lives of others.

So let's take a moment to briefly explore some diverse preaching styles that could potentially help your sermons come to life. Understanding that not every style will work for everyone, each style listed offers a different approach to connecting to the audience and delivering your message effectively. When you combine your preaching style with the divine power of God, incredible outcomes unfold, and lasting impact is made.

- **Expository Preaching**: This style is like diving into a specific part of the Bible, taking it apart bit by bit to understand it inside and out, and sharing your discoveries with the congregation.
- **Topical Preaching**: This is the process of exploring a single topic, like faith or forgiveness, and learning what the Bible says about it. It's like connecting the dots from different parts of the Bible to give a complete picture.

- **Narrative Preaching**: This is the art of telling stories from the Bible in a way that grabs people's attention and helps them see how those stories relate to their own lives.
- **Apologetic Preaching**: This style requires very intentional study. You must be able to explain and defend our Christian faith by using logical and convincing points that address people's doubts and questions.
- **Prophetic Preaching**: This style will always challenge the status quo and urge individuals to align their lives with the will of God. It will consist of speaking the truth, giving guidance, addressing social issues, and calling for personal and societal transformation.
- **Devotional Preaching**: This style gives people practical guidance and encouragement for their daily lives, helping them grow closer to God and live out their faith.
- **Evangelistic Preaching**: This style is solely geared toward sharing the Good News of Jesus and inviting others to experience His redeeming love and salvation for themselves.
- **Dramatic Preaching**: This involves dynamic and engaging sermons that utilize visual tools like demonstrations, illustrations, and even skits to bring a message to life and make it more relatable and memorable.

Are these the only preaching styles? Absolutely not! There are numerous preaching styles beyond the ones listed above. Each style has its unique strengths and can be effective in different contexts. While it's beneficial to develop proficiency in a particular style, versatility can be a tremendous asset as well. Being able to adapt your preaching style to suit the needs of your audience and the message you're delivering is a valuable skill. Always remember that the goal is to communicate the message of the Gospel effectively.

If a different style that is outside of your norm becomes more suitable for a particular service, feel free to use it. The message is what matters most, even when the method changes. Embrace the diversity of preaching styles and use them as tools to reach different audiences and fulfill your ministry's mission.

Keep in mind that preaching style isn't solely based on a

preacher's personality or preferred preference. It's also influenced by the message being delivered and the audience being addressed. So your preaching style can vary depending on the content of your message and the listeners you're connecting with. It's all about being sensitive enough to adapt your approach to the message and the people you're speaking to. Flexibility is key.

Young preacher, you are truly one of a kind with gifts and passions that are all part of God's unique plan. It's up to you to fully embrace your uniqueness and let it shine through your preaching style. When you partner your unique qualities with the power of God, you can make a profound impact on everyone who hears you.

Remember, this calling to preach isn't just about having a stage for a solo performance. It's about making a real difference in the lives of others. With God's guidance and your authentic self, you can truly change the world through your preaching.

However, just reading this chapter alone won't unlock the fullness of the voice you are searching for. Finding your voice is a lifelong journey, and I encourage you to embrace the process of self-discovery and growth more and more. Know that your voice matters and your unique perspectives and experiences have the power to touch hearts and transform lives.

As we journey through this manual, keep pressing forward, continue seeking God's guidance, keep nurturing your unique gifts, and remain true to who you are. In doing so, you will discover the voice that is uniquely yours.

— 99 —

WE HAVE ALL BEEN  BUT THE REASON THEY CAN BE UTILIZED IS DUE TO THE GRACE OF GOD.

— 99 —

Chapter 2

Biblical Foundations

In the previous chapter, we covered important spiritual principles and truths that will help you discover your voice. In this chapter, we'll take a more focused and practical approach to the subject of preaching and the Word of God. Let's dive in!

Preaching should never be about relying on catchphrases and clichés. I think our generation has heard enough of that. Instead, it should be firmly rooted in the timeless wisdom and truth found within the Bible. That is what we preach, stand on, and live by because it is the very Word of God.

The Bible provides a solid foundation for our preaching because it offers depth, richness, and truth that catchphrases can't match. It holds the transformative power we need in our preaching. The Scriptures serve as our guide that shapes our sermons so that when we deliver them, people receive a direct connection to the mind and heart of God. By embracing the truth of the Word, we tap into its life-changing ability and make room for a powerful experience for the congregation.

Second Timothy 3:16 and 17 reminds us, "All Scripture is God-breathed and is useful for teaching, rebuking, correcting and training in righteousness, so that the servant of God may be thoroughly equipped for every good work." As you can see, the Bible is not just any book; it is the very breath of God. It is our ultimate guide and source of wisdom that equips us to teach, correct, and inspire others. But to effectively harness the power of the Word in our preaching, we must dive deep into studying and understanding the Scriptures. By doing so, we can accurately interpret God's message and deliver it with clarity and conviction.

Without knowing how to study the Bible accurately, we open ourselves up to a multitude of consequences that could arise. First, an inaccurate interpretation of the Bible may lead to miscommunication of God's message, which will only cause confusion and misunderstanding among the congregation. Second, it can result in preaching that lacks depth and fails to address the true spiritual needs of the listeners.

Without accurate study, a preacher could unintentionally promote incorrect doctrines or teachings that are harmful to the spiritual and mental health of a congregation. Because of this, we must dedicate time and effort in this manual to covering the importance of studying and understanding the Bible.

This chapter is like a lifelong companion on your preaching journey. You'll find yourself coming back to it time and time again to refine your study practices. Doing so will sharpen your ability to communicate the Word of God with clarity and impact. Let's get started!

Hermeneutics

Hermeneutics is all about interpreting and understanding the Bible; it's the key to unlocking the true meaning of the Word of God. By studying hermeneutics, we gain the principles and methods we need to make sense of what the writers were trying to convey in their writings. It's like having a set of lenses that give us insight into their time and culture. This bridge between the ancient context of the Bible and our modern world allows us to apply its truths to our lives today.

As preachers of the Gospel, our sacred responsibility is to ensure that our delivery of the Scriptures is hermeneutically sound. To effectively communicate the Bible's intended message to our audience, it is crucial that we diligently study and apply hermeneutical principles. This way we can ensure that we convey the true meaning of the Scriptures rather than imposing our own interpretations onto them.

I encourage you to dedicate yourself to presenting God's truth with excellence. Never underestimate the importance of investing time and effort into thorough study. Let that desire to dive into the Scriptures and seek understanding and insights fuel your passion for delivering a powerful and profound message. When you bring all these elements together, you'll be equipped to make a meaningful impact.

It is not lost on me that not everyone comes into ministry with a natural desire to dive into Scripture and dig deep for understanding. And that's okay. The truth is, passion for God's Word doesn't always show up right away—it often develops over time. Life gets busy, and it's easy to feel disconnected, but that doesn't mean you're not called to preach.

Instead, it's a chance to lean into the discipline of studying the Word, knowing that passion often follows commitment. The more time you spend in Scripture, even when you're not "feeling it," the more that desire will grow. Like any meaningful relationship, your connection to God's Word strengthens with time and effort.

If you're struggling to find that hunger, don't be afraid to ask God for it. Scripture says in James 1:5 that if we ask for wisdom, God will give it freely. Start small—meditate on a verse and spend just a few minutes reflecting on what you're reading. It doesn't have to be overwhelming. Little by little, those moments will lead to deeper understanding.

Remember, it's not just about writing a sermon; it's about letting the Word transform you. When you approach Scripture with an open heart, you're meeting with God, and that encounter will naturally fuel your desire to dig even deeper.

Let's take a look at some fundamental principles to remember when it comes to understanding hermeneutics.

- **Context Is Key**: Consider the historical, cultural, and literary context of a passage to understand its true meaning.
- **Author's Intent**: Try to grasp what the original author wanted to communicate through his writing.
- **Take It Literally**: Unless there are clear signs of figurative language, take the text at face value. For example, we take literally John 3:16 (*NKJV*), which says, "For God so loved the world that he gave his one and only Son, that whoever believes in him shall not perish but have eternal life." While we take figuratively John 10:9 where Jesus said, "I am the door." He used figurative language to express that He is *the way* to salvation, not a literal physical door.

- **Know Your Genres**: Recognize that the Bible includes different styles like stories, poetry, and letters. Interpret each genre accordingly.
- **Let Scripture Interpret Scripture**: Use other parts of the Bible to validate your findings within the Scriptures and ensure biblical consistency. Cross-referencing helps us gain a comprehensive understanding of any given verse or subject.

Understanding the principles and methods of hermeneutics is essential for any young preacher. These principles are like the compass that guides our interpretation of the Bible, ensuring that we make it relevant to our lives today. They help us approach the text with the right mindset, allowing us to uncover its true meaning and apply it effectively in our preaching. Without these foundational concepts, our interpretation will be misguided, leading to misunderstandings or misapplications of the Scripture.

Exegesis

There are many methods and study techniques of hermeneutics. *Exegesis* is the process of digging deep into the text to understand the author's intended message to the original audience. This step is crucial because it ensures that our interpretation is rock-solid and faithful to the original context. By mastering exegesis, you can deliver sermons that are not only accurate but are also deeply impactful, resonating with the audience and cultivating a deeper understanding of God's Word.

Let's take a look at some methods for exegesis.

- **Historical-Cultural Context**: This method involves studying the historical and cultural background of the biblical text to better understand its original meaning and relevance to the audience it was written for. For example, in Exodus, you'll find the story of Moses leading the Israelites out of Egypt. Historical-cultural context helps you see the significance of various elements in the story. Knowing that the Israelites were enslaved in Egypt helps you understand the desperation for freedom and the greatness of God's deliverance. Also, knowledge of ancient Egyptian culture and practices helps us know the specific significance of the ten plagues that were sent upon Egypt.

- **Literary Analysis**: By examining the literary features of the Bible, such as genre, structure, and literary devices, preachers can gain insights into the true meaning of the text. Let's take the parable of the prodigal son found in Luke 15 as an example. You can uncover the deeper message of God's love and forgiveness by analyzing the vivid imagery, character development, and plot progression.
- **Language/Word Study**: Understanding the original languages of the Bible, such as Hebrew and Greek, can provide valuable insights into the nuances and meanings of the text. By delving into the specific words, phrases, and grammar used in their original context, you can better understand the intended meaning.

  For example, imagine you're reading the New Testament and see the word "love" in a passage. In English, "love" can mean many different things, but in the original Greek, there are different words for different kinds of love. The Greek word *agape* means *selfless, unconditional love*, while *phileo* means *brotherly love* or *friendship*. Knowing which Greek word was used in a particular verse can help you understand the kind of love being discussed. With that knowledge, let's look at John 21:15-17, where Jesus asks Peter, "...Do you *love* me...?" In Greek, Jesus first uses *agape*, asking if Peter loves Him unconditionally. Peter replied with, "Yes, Lord...You know that I *love* You." But in his reply, he used the Greek word *phileo*, meaning *brotherly love*. This shows the different levels of love and how Peter struggled to say he loved Jesus in the highest way. Understanding these differences can help you explain the passage better and give your audience a deeper understanding of the Bible.
- **Contextual Interpretation**: Considering the broader context of the passage being studied is important. You can

24

understand the context of a verse by exploring the surrounding verses and the book it's a part of as well as considering the Bible as a whole. This will help you avoid misinterpretation and ensure that the sermon aligns with the overall biblical narrative. Let's say someone reads the verse "Money is the root of all evil" from First Timothy 6:10 and interprets it to mean that *all money* is evil. However, when you read the verse in its full context, you see that it actually says, "For *the love* of money is a root of all kinds of evil...." And in case you were wondering, the original Greek word used for "love" in this verse is *philarguria*, which is a derivative of the word *phileo* we learned earlier! This brings *even more* context, doesn't it? The intended message about the dangers of greed and the love of money can be misunderstood by not doing proper contextual interpretation.

- **Theological Framework**: Applying a solid theological framework will help you interpret the Bible in light of its core teachings and doctrines, making sure that your sermon is rooted in sound biblical theology. Start by picking a main theme. Find key Bible passages in both the Old and New Testaments that highlight that main theme.

   For example, look at Genesis 12:1-3 for God's promise to Abraham and Luke 22:20 for the new covenant through Jesus. Next, examine how these passages connect, showing how the theme develops from the Old Testament to the New Testament. Use these connections to build your sermon, creating a story that ties these passages together and shows how God's plan unfolds.

   This approach will help you make your sermons deeply rooted in sound biblical theology and make the Bible's teachings more relatable and understandable for your audience. Basically, building a theological framework helps your message fit into the bigger story of the Bible.

Preaching is not just about putting on a show or using certain verses as props. It's about digging deep into the Scriptures through thorough study and understanding their true meaning.

By subjecting yourself to this kind of study, you ensure that your sermons are rooted in the Bible and convey its intended meaning. This is what helps build a strong foundation for your preaching.

The Significance of Context

Let's look deeper into the significance of context when establishing a solid biblical foundation. Understanding the context of the scriptures we study is like laying a strong foundation for a building—it provides the necessary support and structure for our understanding and interpretation. Without context, our understanding can be prone to misinterpretation, and like a house built on sand, unstable.

Understanding the context of Scripture lays a strong foundation for our biblical understanding and also paves the way for its revelation. When we grasp the context of the Scriptures, we create a solid framework that allows us to receive divine insight and deeper meaning. With context as our guide, we become open to the revelation of Scripture, where God's wisdom and truth are unveiled to us in ways that surpass our human understanding.

When I speak of revelation, I'm referring to the divine unveiling of the meaning and truth of the Word of God. It's the unique "aha" moment when God reveals the deeper layers of understanding beyond our human logic and reasoning. This revelation comes directly from God Himself. However, the true revelation of God's Word is rooted in the foundation of its original context as spoken by God in the Scriptures.

We learned earlier that the process of exegesis is all about finding the original true meaning of a particular verse or passage. There is another term I want you to be familiar with, and that's *eisegesis*. These two words look similar, but they are completely different.

While exegesis is the process of discovering the true meaning of the Word of God, eisegesis is the process of inserting our own opinions and ideas into the text. When you don't know and understand the context of a verse or passage, you run the risk of unintentionally practicing *eisegesis* instead of *exegesis*.

Our job as preachers of the Word of God is not to promote or elevate our opinion but to effectively communicate the Word of God. The power to change lives is found in the Bible—not our opinions.

'By understanding the context in which the Scriptures were written, we can unlock the more profound meaning and significance of God's message. Allow me to explain using a fairly popular verse that is often spoken of or taught out of context:

> **I can do all things through Christ who strengthens me.**
> — **Philippians 4:13** (*NKJV*)

It's common for us to interpret this verse to be about our abilities and potential. We often think it means that we can accomplish anything we set our minds to with Christ's strength. But let's look at this in context to see what revelation God wants to communicate to us through these profound words.

> **Not that I speak in regard to need, for I have learned in whatever state I am, to be content: I know how to be abased, and I know how to abound. Everywhere and in all things I have learned both to be full and to be hungry, both to abound and to suffer need.**
> — **Philippians 4:11,12** (*NKJV*)

Before we look into the significance of Philippians 4:11and 12, let's establish that the apostle Paul wrote this letter while he was in prison. In these verses, Paul expressed his journey of learning to be content in all situations, whether in times of abundance or need. And that's where verse 13 comes in, as Paul emphasized that it is through Christ's strength that he could do all things. Now, let's find the revelation within the context of these verses.

Philippians 4:13 was never about us maximizing our potential and reaching all of our dreams through our abilities. It shows us that through the strength that comes from Christ, we can be content in whatever state we find ourselves in. True contentment and joy come from our relationship with Christ rather than external circumstances. These verses reveal that, in a world filled with distractions and pressures, we should find our strength in Christ to be content in all situations.

As you can see, if we don't consider the context, we risk misinterpreting and diluting the true meaning of Scripture. This can lead to false revelations and misunderstandings. Understanding the context allows you to receive true revelation from God.

We must prioritize understanding the context of any given verse or passage because context grants us access to true revelation. By knowing it, we give God the opportunity to uncover the intended meaning behind the words and how they apply to us today.

So, young preacher, let's never underestimate the power of context in our pursuit of understanding and revelation of God's Word. It's a vital ingredient in building a strong biblical foundation.

Now that we've established the contextual interpretation of Philippians 4:13, let's put the exegetical methods we learned earlier in this chapter in action to see them at work:

Historical-Cultural Context: Philippians is one of the letters written by the apostle Paul while he was in prison, likely in Rome around A.D. 60-62. The city of Philippi was a Roman colony in Macedonia, and the church there was one of the first Christian communities in Europe. The Philippians had a close relationship with Paul, often providing him with financial support. This letter was written to thank them and to encourage them to remain steadfast in their faith despite persecution.

Literary Analysis: Philippians 4:13 is part of a larger section where Paul discussed contentment. In verses 10-20, Paul acknowledged the Philippians' recent gift and explained how he learned to be content in any situation, whether in need or in plenty. The words, "I can do all things through Christ who gives me strength," serve as a powerful conclusion to this section, emphasizing that his ability to endure all circumstances came from Christ.

Language/Word Study: The key phrase in Philippians 4:13 is "I can do all things through Christ who gives me strength." The Greek word for "strength" here is *endynamounti*, which means *to empower* or *to fill with power*. The Greek word for "all things" is *panta* and suggests *a comprehensive scope*, but it is important to interpret it within the context of Paul's discussion on contentment and endurance.

28

Theological Framework: Theologically, Philippians 4:13 highlights the sufficiency of Christ in the believer's life. It underscores the idea that true strength and capability come from reliance on Christ, rather than one's own abilities. This verse is often cited to encourage believers that, regardless of their circumstances, they can rely on Christ's strength to persevere and thrive.

- Other Old and New Testament scriptures that reflect this theological framework:
  - Joshua 1:9 – "Have I not commanded you? Be strong and courageous. Do not be afraid; do not be discouraged, for the Lord your God will be with you wherever you go." This verse encourages strength and courage through God's presence.
  - Psalm 28:7 — "The Lord is my strength and my shield; my heart trusts in him, and he helps me. My heart leaps for joy, and with my song I praise him." This verse reflects the theme of God as a source of strength and protection.
  - Isaiah 40:31 — "But those who hope in the Lord will renew their strength. They will soar on wings like eagles; they will run and not grow weary, they will walk and not be faint." This verse highlights the renewal of strength for those who trust in God.
  - 2 Corinthians 12:9 — "But he said to me, 'My grace is sufficient for you, for my power is made perfect in weakness.' Therefore I will boast all the more gladly about my weaknesses, so that Christ's power may rest on me." This passage emphasizes God's strength being made perfect in our weakness.

In conclusion, Philippians 4:13 is a profound statement of faith that reflects Paul's deep trust in Christ's power to sustain him through all of life's challenges.

As you can see, developing good study habits and seeking to truly understand the Bible are essential for any preacher who wants to communicate God's Word accurately. It's not just about getting through the text—it's about letting the text get through to you.

When you invest time in careful study, prayer, and reflection, you equip yourself to rightly handle the Word of truth. Your ability to faithfully represent what God is saying depends on your commitment to knowing His Word inside and out. This kind of dedication not only strengthens your preaching but also deepens your relationship with God, allowing His message to flow through you with clarity and power.

—  —

Never

UNDERESTIMATE THE IMPORTANCE OF INVESTING TIME AND EFFORT INTO THOROUGH STUDY.

— 99 —

Chapter 3

Crafting Compelling Sermons

Any preacher should aim to excel in *readiness* and *preparation*. These two elements set the stage for delivering impactful sermons that speak directly to the hearts of the congregation. Being thoroughly prepared not only ensures a clear and compelling delivery but also allows the preacher to connect with the audience on a deeper level, fostering a more profound understanding and connection with the sermon.

The Bible truly guides preachers on the vital role of readiness and preparation when delivering a message. Second Timothy 2:4 stresses the importance of being prepared at all times, whether in or out of season. This wisdom emphasizes the continual readiness required for preachers to share God's Word effectively, showcasing the commitment needed to deliver the message regardless of the circumstances they encounter. It highlights the significance of consistently delivering the message with impact, even when faced with challenges or inconveniences.

Crafting a compelling sermon involves weaving together elements like a well-selected theme, a structured outline, engaging illustrations, and storytelling techniques. When a preacher masters preparedness, he or she can effectively communicate the sermon with passion, clarity, and relevance, creating a powerful connection with the listeners and leaving a lasting impact.

By understanding this, we can delve deeper into crafting a compelling sermon. Just as being ready at all times is crucial for effective preaching, preparing and structuring a sermon plays a vital role in engaging and connecting with the congregation.

Selecting a Theme

Selecting a theme that truly resonates with the audience is like syncing up with God to convey His message in its purest form. It's all about connecting with the core of God's wisdom to understand what will both stir and captivate the hearts of the hearers.

When God unveils that wisdom, it's not just about giving a sermon; it's about crafting a sanctuary where hearts unfurl, minds stir, and lives embark on a journey of change. That's when the real power of your sermon radiates, guiding the listeners toward a revelation and motivation that endures well past the closing "amen."

Before we learn how to select a theme for a message, let's briefly discuss the difference between the *theme* of a sermon and the *title* of the sermon. Although they are closely intertwined, they are not the same. The *title* is more like the "face" of the sermon, giving a concise snapshot of what the sermon is about. On the other hand, the *theme* sets the tone and overarching message of the sermon. The *theme* delves deeper into the substance, while the *title* acts as a beacon that draws the congregation in.

Choosing a theme for your sermon can seem like a big task, but it doesn't have to be complicated. Here are a few steps to help you figure it out:

1. **Pray**: Before you even *start* thinking about what you're going to preach, pray. Ask God to guide your thoughts and show you what He wants you to speak about. You're not just picking a theme; you're delivering God's message, so prayer is essential.

2. **Dig Into the Bible**: Spend time in Scripture. You'll notice that certain passages, ideas, or stories will jump out at you. That's often a clue as to what your theme should be. Let the Bible inspire and direct you.

3. **Think About Your Audience**: Your congregation or audience has real needs. Are they struggling with doubt, dealing with difficult relationships, or needing encouragement? When you know where they are spiritually, it's easier to focus on a theme that speaks directly to them.

4. **Don't Overcomplicate It**: It's tempting to want to cover many things at once, but you should resist that urge. Stick to one clear idea. If your theme is "faith," don't try to also cover "hope" and "love" in the same message. Focusing on one theme brings clarity and depth to your message.

5. **Point to Jesus**: Whatever theme you land on, remember to

keep it centered on Jesus. The goal of any sermon is to lead people closer to Him, so make sure your theme connects to the Gospel and points people in that direction.

Let's take a moment in this section to briefly shift our focus and consider a viewpoint from the perspective of a guest minister invited to preach. There may be instances where the host has already chosen a theme for the event. In such cases, it becomes your responsibility as the invited preacher to seek God's guidance and craft a sermon based on the theme provided by the host. I want to take a moment to highlight the significance of matching your sermon with the host's theme and the essential aspect of seeking God's inspiration in preparing your sermon.

As a guest preacher, you might feel at times that God is leading you in a different direction than what is given by the host. In situations like these, the first step is to respect the host's vision. The host has invited you as part of his or her broader plan for the congregation, and it's important to honor that plan by considering the request seriously. Preaching outside of the theme without consulting the host could disrupt the flow that has been previously established.

However, if you sense God giving you a different theme, take it to prayer for clarity. Ask God whether this is truly the message for that specific occasion, or if it's meant for another time. Often, God will provide a way to align your message with the theme the host has asked for, even if it doesn't seem clear at first. Sometimes the themes may be more connected than you realized, and through prayer, you'll see how to weave the two together.

If after praying you still feel led to preach a different message, it's important to communicate with the host. Let him or her know what's on your heart and why you feel God is leading you this way. Most hosts will appreciate your openness and may allow you to follow that direction. At the same time, be willing to find a compromise that honors both the leading of the Holy Spirit and the theme the host has set. Ultimately, remember that God's Word is broad and interconnected, and His truth will come through as long as your heart is focused on glorifying Him.

Sermon themes revolve around topics like love, victory, forgiveness, hope, faith, perseverance, etc. For instance, a theme on forgiveness could be communicated in a sermon entitled "Embracing Grace" or "The Power of Forgiveness," and a sermon with a theme on hope might be entitled "Finding Light in Darkness" or "Unwavering Hope."

As you can see, a strong theme is like a light that illuminates the path for both the preacher and the congregation. It encapsulates the essence of the sermon being communicated to the people. So to determine a title for your sermon, you must first lock in on the theme.

The Importance of Clarity and Relevance

Selecting a clear and relevant theme helps your message connect with your congregation effectively. When your theme is easy to understand and directly related to what you're sharing, it makes a stronger impact on who you're sharing the message with. So clarity and relevance in theme selection are vital to delivering a powerful and meaningful sermon.

When selecting a theme, it's important to choose something that can be easily understood and straightforward. It should be seen throughout the entirety of your sermon. Without a clear theme, the congregation cannot easily grasp the essence of your message.

Have you ever heard a sermon and left wondering, "What did the preacher talk about?" If so, it's because no clear theme was communicated throughout the message. For the sermon to be understood by the hearer, the main point must be crystal clear. Having a clear theme is like providing a roadmap. It guides the audience directly to the heart of your message without any confusion.

Imagine a sermon with the theme "Love and Kindness." In this sermon, every point and story shared revolves around showing love and kindness to others. The congregation can easily follow along and understand the central message of spreading love and kindness. There's no room for confusion, and there's a simple and direct focus that helps communicate the message clearly and effectively.

The other critical piece of crafting an impactful sermon and choosing a theme is relevance. Relevance in theme selection for sermons means choosing topics that directly connect with the congregation's lives, experiences, and needs. Selecting a relevant theme helps grab the congregation's attention by speaking to their real-life situations. But the question remains: How can a preacher determine the relevance of a theme?

Firstly, the preacher must seek God's guidance through prayer and preparation to understand the congregation's current needs and the season they are in. This helps in selecting themes that align with what the congregation requires at that specific time.

Secondly, a preacher can determine the relevance of a theme by considering the congregation's current challenges, struggles, and joys. By understanding the people's experiences and emotions, the preacher can choose themes that directly connect with the listeners, making the message more relatable and engaging.

Picking a theme that is relevant to the congregation makes it easier for everyone to relate to the message. Relatability helps the congregation connect with the message on a personal level. It enables you to "speak their language" and keep them engaged. Through this, a deeper connection between the message and the listeners is established.

If a preacher talks about dealing with struggles at school and most of the congregation consists of students, that relatable theme would likely get everyone nodding along and thinking about how to apply the sermon to their lives; the theme is relevant to them. When the sermon theme hits close to home for the congregation, it's easier for them to see how they can use the message in their everyday lives.

Creating an Organized Outline

When creating your semon outline for a clear and organized flow, it's essential to have a structured approach. While various preaching styles exist (like we discussed earlier in the manual), I believe each sermon must possess a well-defined outline to serve as the foundation for its delivery.

A sermon outline provides a clear roadmap for the preacher, ensuring that the message is organized and flows smoothly. A well-organized structure is like the backbone of a sermon, holding everything together and keeping it strong. It helps you stay on track, ensuring your message is clear and easy to follow. Let's look deeper.

INTRODUCTION

When developing a sermon introduction, it's essential to create an engaging opening that hooks the listeners, sets the sermon's tone, and states the purpose and theme of your message. For a good introduction, you'll want to have at least one, if not all, of the following components:

Hook: Think of it like reeling in your audience with something attention grabbing, like a story, a powerful quote, or a thought provoking question that makes everyone sit up and take notice. It's about getting them interested and excited to hear more.

Context: This sets the stage for what you're going to share. You can provide background information, paint a picture of the situation in the text, or explain why your theme is important. This helps the listeners understand where you're coming from and why your message matters.

Thesis Statement: This is the main point or big idea you want to convey in your sermon. It's the central message that you want everyone to remember. It's a summary of what your sermon is all about, and it guides the direction of your message

Transition: This is the art of smoothly moving from one idea to the next. Specifically, within the introduction, it's the bridge that connects it to the body of your sermon, preparing the listeners for what's to come.

MAIN POINTS

To break down a sermon into main points, you can start by identifying the key messages you want to convey to your audience. Think about what you want them to take away from your sermon then organize your sermon into distinct sections or points that address these key messages.

Each section should focus on a specific idea or theme related to your overall message. By breaking down your sermon into main sections or points, you can ensure your message is clear, organized, and impactful to your listeners.

Let's use a sermon about forgiveness as an example. Here's how we would structure the main points for that:

Main Points:
1. Understanding Forgiveness
2. Forgiving Others
3. Seeking Forgiveness

When laying out your main points, remember to include elements that support what you're trying to say. These pieces are crucial to strengthening the message you're delivering.

Think of supporting details, illustrations, and relevant scriptures for each point in your sermon as the key pieces that make your message strong and exciting. Supporting details help explain and validate your main points, while illustrations bring your message to life and make it easy to understand. Adding relevant scriptures gives your message a solid base and makes it more meaningful. Including these elements in your sermon makes it more engaging and powerful for your audience.

You also want to connect all your main points smoothly in your sermon. This connection between each point helps create a cohesive flow throughout your message, making it easier for your audience to follow. Ensuring a logical progression from one point to the next in your sermon is like building a bridge that connects each idea smoothly. You want your audience to feel as if they're taking a natural and effortless journey through your message, where each point naturally leads to the next.

In creating this seamless flow, you help your listeners grasp the bigger picture and understand how each point fits into the overall message you're sharing. It's all about guiding them through your sermon in a clear and engaging way.

Subpoints and Transitions

Let's have a deeper discussion about these two components of a sermon: *subpoints* and *transitions*. When developing subpoints under each main point in your sermon, you should include supporting details that expand on and clarify your main ideas. Subpoints help break down the main points into smaller, more digestible pieces, making your message easier to follow and understand. It's like breaking a big task into smaller steps to make it more manageable and clear for your audience.

This approach allows you to thoroughly explore each aspect of your main points, ensuring that your message is well-organized and easy to follow. Consider including examples, illustrations, stories, or quotes to elaborate on each subpoint and provide depth to your sermon. This will enhance the overall clarity and impact of your message.

To make it clearer, let's take the sermon on forgiveness we discussed earlier and see what details should be covered in our subpoints:

Sermon About Forgiveness

Main Points:

1. Understanding Forgiveness
   Subpoints
   Quotes, examples, scriptures, and illustrations that
   help define forgiveness and its impact on personal growth.

2. Forgiving Others
   Subpoints
   Share supporting details to show the healing it brings to
   both parties.

3. Seeking Forgiveness
   Subpoints
   Evidence that highlights the importance of seeking forgiveness and reconciliation in relationships.

As we discussed briefly, when it comes to smoothly connecting different sections in your sermon, your transitions are the bridges that guide your audience from one idea to the next without any "bumps." These transitions help maintain a logical flow and keep your listeners engaged throughout the sermon. By using simple phrases like "moving on to our next point" or "building on what we just discussed," you can link each section together for a cohesive and easy-to-follow presentation.

In the sermon about forgiveness, you could use phrases like, "Now that we've grasped an understanding of forgiveness, let's shift our focus to forgiveness in a broader context," or, "Let's move on from understanding the impact of forgiving others to discussing the importance of seeking forgiveness for our own mistakes." These transitions help smoothly guide your audience from one aspect of forgiveness to the next, creating a unified flow.

For the subpoints and transitions to maintain a cohesive flow throughout your outline, you must ensure that each subpoint logically connects to the main point it supports. By using transitions between subpoints, you can guide your audience through a structured journey of your sermon.

Application and Conclusion

Including practical application in your sermon is crucial because it helps your audience understand how to implement the teachings in their everyday lives. It is those lessons that they can apply to real-life situations. The practical application makes the message relevant and actionable, promoting personal growth and transformation. It answers questions like, "How can I apply this message in my life?" or, "What specific actions can I take to live out this sermon?"

In that same sermon about forgiveness, the practical application could involve encouraging an understanding of forgiveness by reflecting on personal experiences, forgiving others by practicing empathy and compassion, and seeking forgiveness through honest communication and reconciliation. These practical examples will help your listeners apply the message in their daily lives.

To make the practical application work, you need to sum up the sermon's main points. This is where you reiterate the main points discussed, highlight the key messages, and emphasize the practical application of the teachings. By doing this, you ensure that everyone clearly understands what was shared and how they can apply it.

To end your sermon with a powerful conclusion that reinforces the central theme and resonates with the audience, you can offer a final thought or challenge related to the theme and leave the congregation with a sense of inspiration or motivation to apply the teachings in their lives. This kind of conclusion can leave a lasting impact and make the sermon memorable.

To conclude the sermon on forgiveness, you might emphasize its transformative power and how it can lead to personal growth, healing, and a sense of peace. This would leave the congregation with a message of hope and the importance of extending forgiveness to others.

There's much more to explore about crafting engaging sermons and boosting their impact. We'll delve into those topics in the upcoming chapter. However, nailing down a suitable theme for your sermon and crafting a well-structured outline are essential for guiding the congregation toward enlightenment and transformation.

Young preacher, remember that each sermon you craft is a chance to inspire, connect, and uplift. Embrace the journey of honing your preparation and structure skills. Your passion and dedication will shine through as you impact others with your message.

To help bring everything we've discussed in this chapter to life, I've included one of my own sermons as an example. This sermon is meant to demonstrate how the principles we've covered can be applied in real-life preaching. As you review it, pay attention to the flow, transitions, and how each point is built upon Scripture. My hope is that this example gives you practical insight into crafting impactful sermons of your own.

The following sermon was preached during the Advent season as part of a series titled *Advent: Backstage Access*. In this series, we explored the lives of key figures in the Christmas story and the birth of Jesus Christ, extracting principles we can apply to our daily lives.

Mary: The Womb God Wants
Luke 1:27-35,38

- Nazareth was an unremarkable, plain place.
  - No one took pride in being a Nazarene.
  - Fewer than 2,000 people were from Nazareth.
  - The Romans kept a regional fortress there. Therefore, the place was considered unclean by most Jews.
    - When the town produced a new Teacher (Jesus), the

hometown was on strike against him.

- John 1:46 *KJV* — "And Nathanael said unto him, Can there any good thing come out of Nazareth?"
  - o Nazareth was Jewish by birthright, Roman by claim, and Greek by influence.
  - o It was a quiet town, and if you wanted excitement, you would have to walk four miles up the road to Sepphoris, which was a city that kept up with the latest Greek culture.
- Mary seems to have been a very typical young lady from a typical small town (proof from Luke's style of writing).
  - o Despite this, Mary seems to have been living the dream life of any young girl.
    - She was engaged to a young carpenter. She and Joseph were ready to begin their adult life.
  - o Mary's life was filled with preparation for what would be a big day in her life.
    - Exchanging of gifts by the family, the joy of a wedding ceremony, the opportunity to wear jewelry and fine clothes, and, finally, she would leave her home.
  - o Mary had to have gone through life fulfilling these preparations with a happy heart. Those were the final days as a young maiden.
- In the midst of her routine, a single supernatural encounter shattered the normality of her life.
  - o Whenever the supernatural invades your life, it comes to interrupt what you always knew.
- Luke 1:28 — "The angel went to her and said, 'Greetings, one who is highly favored. The Lord is with you.'"
  - o Mary is seen as average and typical by men, but she's seen as highly favored by God.
    - The perspective of men does not determine the amount of favor on your life.
  - o Mary had been made to seem so average that even she became perplexed at what Gabriel said (*see* Luke 1:29).
- vv. 30,31 *NKJV* — "...The angel said to her, 'Do not be afraid Mary, for you have found favor with God. And behold, you will conceive in your womb and bring forth a Son, and shall call His

name Jesus.'"

- o Because of all the favor on her life given by God, she was going to conceive and bear a Son.
- o Problem: She was a virgin and was not married.
  - Favor from God would look like fornication to the public.
  - This would cause her to potentially be stoned, according to the law.
    - It is true that favor isn't fair, but you can't say that and not realize that favor also does cost something.
    - Favor is meant to advance God's plan, not just make your life easier.
      - o Favor requires responsibility.
    - The cost of favor is faithfulness and the courage to follow God, even when it's hard, knowing that His favor always comes with purpose and a greater reward in the end.
- v. 34 — "Mary said to the angel, 'How can this be, since I am a virgin?'"
- v. 35 — "The angel said to her, 'The Holy Spirit will come on you, and the power of the Most High will overshadow you....'"
  - o This birthing would not happen like the typical birth; this would not require the assistance of man.
  - o This birth would happen by the power of the Holy Ghost.
- The question is: Why would God choose Mary of all people?
  - o The answer lies in verse 38.
  - o Even though Mary didn't understand what was happening nor how it was going to happen, her devotion to God prompted her to say, "Be it unto me according to thy word."
    - God wants to use individuals who have committed themselves to being available to Him, even when they don't fully understand what is happening or how things will unfold.

— 99 —

WHEN A PREACHER *masters* PREPAREDNESS, HE OR SHE CAN EFFECTIVELY COMMUNICATE THE SERMON WITH PASSION, CLARITY, AND RELEVANCE...

— 99 —

Chapter 4

Connecting With Your Audience

The apostle Paul set a great example for us on how to effectively minister to others. In First Corinthians 9:22, Paul said that he had become all things to all people so that by all possible means he might save some. Paul expressed his willingness to adapt and relate to different people in various ways to reach them with the message of salvation. He aimed to connect with others on their level to increase the chances of sharing the Gospel effectively and saving souls.

Paul's message reminds us preachers of the importance in being adaptable and empathetic when sharing our faith. First Corinthians 9:22 encourages us to meet people where they are, understand their perspectives, and communicate the message of salvation in a way that resonates with them. This verse shows us the value of building connections and relationships to share the message of Jesus Christ effectively.

Just like Paul aimed to connect with different people to bring them salvation, we, too, need to grasp the importance of connecting with our audiences on various levels to effectively share the message of the Gospel. Being a masterful communicator, Paul showed us the impact of reaching hearts through effective communication. We should aim to follow that example by honing our communication skills to convey the Gospel message.

Effective communication helps connect with the congregation and makes the message more relatable and engaging. Mastering communication skills can significantly enhance your ability to deliver a message effectively and impactfully. Effective communication isn't just about what comes out of your mouth; it's about using your whole self to connect with the congregation. Your body language, tone of voice, and presence all play a role in delivering your message. Let's take a moment and give attention to this subject.

The Art of Effective Communication

When I talk about effective communication as an art, I am referring to being mindful that every action, every word, and every expression you use comes together to deliver your message with clarity and power. It's about engaging your audience with your whole self to share the message in a way that truly resonates with them.

Every great preacher should aim to be a great communicator. Being a great communicator goes beyond just delivering a message; it's about using your entire being to connect with your congregation on a deeper level, inspiring them, and helping them understand and apply the message in their lives. When a preacher excels at communication, he or she has the ability to touch hearts, change lives, and make a lasting impact on those who hear the message being preached.

Body Language

You may find it hard to believe that body language can drastically impact your effectiveness as a preacher. Let me show you how poor body language can hold you back from connecting with your listeners.

Poor body language for a preacher during a sermon can include closed-off gestures like crossed arms, excessive fidgeting, slouching, avoiding eye contact, or displaying distracting facial expressions. Negative body language cues can hinder the preacher's connection with the congregation, undermine the message delivery, and create barriers to effective communication. It's essential for young preachers to be mindful of their body language to ensure they are effectively engaging their congregation during their sermons.

Body language is about our nonverbal signals through gestures, facial expressions, and posture. For preachers, using body language effectively means being aware of how these cues can help them engage their listeners, build rapport, and deliver their message with impact and authenticity. Body language complements verbal communication to convey sincerity and connection, acting as the silent partner to our words.

It's all about moving, standing, and expressing ourselves without speaking. When we use positive body language while preaching, it adds depth and authenticity to our words. So combining verbal and nonverbal cues helps us communicate more effectively and build a genuine bond with our listeners.

Here are some ways you can use body language effectively:

- Maintain good posture to demonstrate conviction in the message.
- Use hand and arm gestures to emphasize key points and engage the audience
- Express emotions through facial expressions to convey authenticity, empathy, joy, or seriousness.
- Utilize eye contact to connect with individuals in the congregation (we'll talk more about this later).

Here are some body-language cues you should avoid if your goal is to be impactful in your delivery:

- Slouching or fidgeting, which can convey a lack of confidence.
- Distracting gestures that take away from the message
- Staring or looking disinterested.
- Facial expressions that don't align with the message being delivered.

I encourage you, young preacher, to see practicing and being mindful of your nonverbal cues as a way to level up your preaching. Like practicing a sermon, honing your body language skills takes time and effort.

To help, try recording yourself and practicing in front of the mirror to see how you come across visually. Being intentional about your nonverbal cues can enhance your communication and create a more engaging and impactful preaching experience for your audience.

Vocal Variety

Vocal variety in preaching means changing how you speak to keep your audience interested. It involves adjusting your delivery's pitch, speed, loudness, and emotions to enhance your message and keep your audience interested and connected. If applied correctly, good vocal variety will keep the listeners on the edge of their seats, eager to hear more.

Vocal variety can also be applied when ministering to different age groups. Speaking in a way that resonates with each age group can help keep everyone attentive and connected during the sermon. Think about it like this: you must customize your speaking style to fit the audience you're addressing.

For a better understanding, here are the types of vocal variety found in most preaching styles:

- **Pitch**: This is the act of changing the highness or lowness of your voice. You can go high for excitement and low for seriousness.
- **Pace**: This describes the speed at which you speak. Slow down to emphasize important points and speed up to keep things lively.
- **Volume**: This is another word for how loud or soft you speak. Use loudness to grab attention and softness to create intimacy.
- **Tone**: Describes the emotion behind your words. Adjust your tone to match the mood of your message, like being joyful, serious, or empathetic.

When you incorporate vocal variety in your preaching, you gain awesome advantages. For instance, it helps grab people's attention and hold their interest. By making the proper adjustments in your delivery, you can keep your audience engaged throughout your sermon. Also, it helps people grasp and remember the important points better by making sure your words are clear and memorable. Lastly, it creates a lively and captivating style in your preaching by adding excitement and depth to your message.

Vocal variety is not just about natural talent. It's a skill that young preachers need to work on and practice with the proper techniques. By honing their abilities in using different tones, speeds, volumes, and emotions, young preachers can truly master the art of engaging an audience with their voice.

Here's a list of some techniques you can practice to improve vocal variety:

- Practice vocal warm-ups and exercises.
- Record and listen to yourself preaching to identify areas in need of improvement.
- Incorporate pauses and silence for dramatic effect.
- Experiment with different tones, pitches, and volumes.

I hope you see how crucial of an element vocal variety is in your preaching. It helps keep your audience connected to your message. By mastering the different components of vocal variety, you can effectively convey your message and make a lasting impact on your listeners. It's all about doing what's necessary to create a dynamic and engaging experience for your congregation.

Eye Contact

There's nothing worse than when a preacher gets so focused on the sermon notes that he or she forgets to make eye contact with the congregation. If a preacher never makes eye contact during the sermon, the danger is that it can create a sense of disconnect and disengagement.

Eye contact plays a vital role in connecting with the congregation during preaching. It helps establish trust, engagement, and connection with the audience. When preachers make eye contact, it shows attentiveness and sincerity, making the sermon more impactful and relatable to the listeners.

Additionally, eye contact enhances a preacher's credibility with the audience. Maintaining eye contact shows that the preacher is engaged and committed to delivering the message and therefore boosting the preacher's credibility in the eyes of the congregation.

Meaningful eye contact creates a sense of authenticity and trust, making the message more believable. Because it makes the message more believable, eye contact ultimately causes the listeners to feel more involved with the message being shared. The listeners then gain the perception of the preacher as being genuine, trustworthy, and relatable.

You can maintain eye contact effectively by scanning the room and briefly connecting with various individuals. Focus on one person for just a couple of seconds, then smoothly transition to another. Be mindful not to linger too long on any one person. Prolonged eye contact may make people feel uncomfortable. The goal is to make everyone feel included and engaged without singling anyone out or creating an awkward moment.

Eye contact can also convey emotions and emphasize key points in the sermon. When expressing heartfelt moments or important messages, looking directly at the congregation helps you connect with the audience on a deeper level, making the emotions and key points more memorable.

Eye contact is crucial not only for the preacher but also for the listener. Think of eye contact as what connects you with your congregation during the sermon. You're not just speaking to the crowd; you're building a personal connection with each person in the audience. This connection makes your message more powerful and creates a shared experience that enhances your sermons overall delivery and reception.

When a preacher masters body language, vocal variety, and eye contact, a strong foundation for effective communication is created. These elements engage the audience, convey emotions, and build a genuine connection that will ultimately lead to many lives being changed.

Tailoring Sermons

Tailoring sermons is simply customizing a message to fit a specific audience or situation. It's about crafting a sermon that resonates with the people you're speaking to, addressing their needs, concerns, and experiences. By tailoring sermons, preachers can make their messages more relatable and powerful for the listeners. When you manage to connect with people of all ages and diverse cultural backgrounds, that's when the sermon truly hits home.

Different Age Groups

Tailoring sermons to different age groups allows preachers to connect with the congregation intentionally. By understanding the characteristics and preferences of various age groups, preachers can deliver messages that resonate with each group's unique needs and interests. This personalized approach enhances the sermon's engagement, comprehension, and overall impact, creating a more meaningful experience for the congregation. It shows that the preacher values and respects the diversity within the congregation, fostering a sense of inclusivity and relevance in the message being shared.

In my time in ministry, I've discovered key elements within different age groups that make sermons more impactful. Let me share a few things I've learned.

For Children (3 to 12 years old):
When tailoring sermons for children, make the message engaging and understandable for their age group. Using storytelling, interactive elements, and simple language can help capture their attention and make the sermon more relatable. By incorporating fun activities and visual aids, preachers can create a memorable and impactful experience for the young ones in the congregation.

For Teenagers (13 to 19 years old):
When tailoring sermons for teenagers, it's important to address topics relevant to their lives and interests. Engaging them with interactive discussions, relatable examples, and opportunities for them to express their thoughts can help create a connection and make the sermon more impactful. Focusing on real-life challenges and providing guidance on navigating adolescence helps the preacher effectively reach out to this age group.

For Young Adults (20 to 39 years old):
When tailoring sermons for young adults, you can delve into topics that resonate with them, like career, relationships, and personal growth. Encouraging discussion, providing practical

advice, and incorporating relevant examples from daily life can help engage young adults and make the sermon more meaningful to them. It's about connecting with them on a level that speaks to their life experiences and aspirations.

For Middle-Aged Adults (40 to 59 years old):

Be sure to address themes like family dynamics, finding purpose in midlife, and navigating life's challenges. Offering guidance, making space for moments of reflection, and providing a sense of community can help you connect with this age group in their stage in life.

For Seniors (60 years old and up):

When ministering to seniors, it's crucial to remind them that there is still purpose and meaning in their lives. Addressing themes like finding strength and hope, wisdom, legacy, and faith in later stages of life helps the preacher connect with their life experiences and journeys as seniors. This also helps bring them more comfort and inspiration.

Be mindful that you may often have more than one age group in your audience, so it's important for young preachers to connect with everyone at their level purposefully. Therefore, when tailoring sermons for different age groups, you must acknowledge your audience's diverse needs and experiences. To connect effectively with all listeners, regardless of age, understanding each group's unique perspectives should be part of your preparation process. By showing empathy, respect, and relevance in your sermon, you'll create connections beyond age barriers and speak to the hearts of all individuals in the congregation. It's all about embracing diversity and making everyone feel seen and valued during the sermon experience.

Different Cultural Backgrounds

The initial step for a preacher in tailoring sermons for various cultural backgrounds is to recognize the diverse cultural mix within the audience. After all, you can't effectively minister to what you're unaware of in your congregation.

In one church, you may find a mix of cultural backgrounds such as African American, Hispanic, Asian, Middle Eastern, and European, each bringing their unique traditions, values, and perspectives to the congregation. You must recognize and celebrate the richness that different cultures bring to the sermon experience. By embracing cultural diversity, you can create a more inclusive and meaningful message that speaks to a wide range of individuals in your audience.

That's why it's vital to do thorough research and be aware of the diverse cultural backgrounds you will be ministering to. Researching the cultural backgrounds in your congregation helps you grasp your listeners better while being aware of the cultural norms, values, and traditions that could impact how your message is received and enables you to tailor your message effectively for a better connection.

Take, for example, a preacher who prepares a sermon on the concept of faith. To truly connect with the diverse congregation, the preacher must delve into the community's different cultural interpretations of faith. By understanding and respecting these various perspectives, the preacher can deliver a message that speaks to each individual, making it more impactful and inclusive. This leads me to my next point: adaptation and inclusivity.

Adaptation is when something changes to fit a specific situation or group of people. *Inclusivity* is making sure everyone feels welcome and included, regardless of background or differences. In sermon preparation, adaptation and inclusivity ensure that the entire congregation understands the message.

By adapting the sermon to cater to the diverse cultural backgrounds present in the church, the preacher can make everyone feel included and valued. To accomplish this, you can incorporate stories, examples, and references that resonate with the different cultural groups. This creates a welcoming and enriching worship experience for everyone involved.

Additionally, being mindful of language and communication is an effective way to ensure your presentation resonates with your listeners. In your sermon preparation, consider the diverse backgrounds of the congregation by using inclusive language that all members easily understand. When you use complex language or references that the people don't understand, you will alienate some church members and cause them to struggle with connecting with the sermon. Remember this note: preaching is about something other than how smart you can sound. Instead, it's about how impactful you can be. Whenever you have a good comprehension of the cultural nuances in communication styles, you can adjust accordingly to truly reach the audience.

As a young preacher, your goal should be to build bridges every time you mount the pulpit. By this, I mean you must purpose in your heart to build bridges in your sermons. You must focus on fostering connections and understanding among different cultural backgrounds within the congregation. By intentionally acknowledging and celebrating diversity, you can create a welcoming and inclusive church community where everyone feels valued and respected.

The Power of Storytelling

Storytelling has been a fundamental part of human communication since ancient times. It began as a way for early civilizations to pass down knowledge, traditions, and cultural values from generation to generation. In the earliest days, stories were shared orally around campfires, in caves, and through other forms of oral tradition. These tales served as entertainment and as a means of preserving history and teaching important lessons.

Over time, storytelling evolved and took on different forms, such as written books and novels, theater, and digital storytelling. So as you can see, the art of storytelling has deep roots in our human experience and continues to play a significant role in our society, including in our preaching.

The concept of storytelling is important for young preachers to discuss because stories have the power to capture attention and drive home important messages in a way that connects with diverse audiences. Mastering the art of storytelling enhances your communication skills and ability to convey the truths of the Bible in a compelling manner. Embracing this concept in sermons can transform a simple message into a memorable and transformative experience for the preacher and the congregation.

Mark 4:33 and 34 (*NIV*) says, "With many similar parables Jesus spoke the word to them, as much as they could understand. He did not say anything to them without using a parable. But when he was alone with his own disciples, he explained everything." Here, we witness Jesus, the master storyteller, using parables to impart truths to His disciples and the crowds that followed Him. Just as Jesus conveyed deep spiritual insights through relatable stories, modern-day preachers can harness the power of storytelling to connect with the listeners on a personal level. Through the art of storytelling, we have the privilege of inviting the congregation into a narrative that not only captivates their hearts but also illuminates wisdom.

As we go deeper into this discussion, let's take inspiration from Mark 4:34 and strive to craft narratives that don't just entertain but also *edify*. Let's tell stories that not only engage but also *enlighten*. Looking at Jesus' example, we see how He used storytelling, or *parables*, to capture people's interest and keep them focused on what He was saying. In the same way, we can use storytelling to bring messages to life in a way that "clicks" with those who listen.

Sometimes, explaining a concept through a story can make it more understandable than a list of facts. Sure, having facts is fantastic, but what's the use of throwing out facts without making things clear? As mentioned earlier, stories help simplify complex ideas and make them easier to grasp. When things are clear and easy to understand, they really stick in people's minds.

When talking about memorability, we're focusing on creating a lasting impression on the hearts of your listeners. Storytelling plays a crucial role in enhancing that impression by presenting your information in narrative form. By structuring key points as stories, they become more engaging and relatable to the audience, increasing the likelihood of their remembering the message.

The storytelling approach assists in making even the most complex information flow smoothly, free of any confusion. This will help inspire, motivate, comfort, and challenge your audience in a way that pure facts may not.

Here are just a few tips to level-up your storytelling in sermons:

- Use everyday stories that people can relate to.

- Make stories vivid with exciting details and conversations.
- Share your own experiences to connect better with the listeners.
- Link your biblical text to a modern-day story 'to showcase the power and relatability of the Word of God.
- Use stories and examples from different cultures to connect with everyone in the church.
- Adjust your speaking style to reach out effectively to people from various backgrounds.

In essence, the stories you share have a unique way of creating a shared experience among the listeners. By weaving personal experiences and relatable narratives into your sermons, you're making a sense of connection and understanding within the congregation.

Connecting with your audience through effective communication, tailoring sermons, and storytelling is like crafting a masterpiece of understanding. Engaging with your audience is not just about words; it's about utilizing your entire being and recognizing the diverse backgrounds of your listeners to create a space where everyone feels valued and understood.

So, young preacher, I would encourage you to be intentional about connecting with your audience by approaching each sermon with a goal of "becoming all things to all people," according to First Corinthians 9:22 *NKJV*. Take the time to understand the cultural backgrounds, beliefs, and experiences of those you're addressing. Show genuine interest in their stories and perspectives, and let the wisdom of God guide you in how to communicate the message to them in a clear way.

Remember, your words have the power to inspire, uplift, and heal. Stay true to yourself, be receptive to learning from others, and always speak from the heart of God. Your sincerity in connecting with your audience will resonate deeply and make a profound impression on your audience. So keep finding those ways to connect with your audience. They need your compassion and wisdom.

— 99 —

EFFECTIVE COMMUNICATION ISN'T JUST ABOUT WHAT COMES OUT OF YOUR MOUTH; IT'S ABOUT USING YOUR WHOLE SELF TO connect WITH THE CONGREGATION.

— 99 —

Chapter 5

Navigating Difficult Topics

Sin. Sexuality. Race. Mental health. Divorce. Alcohol. Marijuana. Abortion. Politics. These topics and more could be classified as "taboo" due to the sensitivity and differing opinions surrounding them. Discussing issues such as these can stir up strong emotions and beliefs. Even still, the role of a preacher in addressing controversial topics through the Word of God is weighty responsibility. As a preacher, you must shed light on challenging issues, offering wisdom and guidance rooted in the teachings of the Bible.

By approaching these topics with love and compassion, preachers can create a safe space for discussion and reflection among their congregation. This shows the intentionality of sharing God's truth in a way that uplifts and edifies. When preachers navigate controversial subjects with care, they not only impart valuable insights but also demonstrate the power of love in addressing difficult conversations.

Ephesians 4:15 is a specific scripture that will be the focal point for the entirety of this chapter.

But speaking the truth in love, [we] may grow up in all things into Him who is the head—Christ.

Ephesians 4:15 serves as a valuable guide for young preachers navigating challenging topics. This verse emphasizes the importance of speaking truthfully while demonstrating care and empathy. It encourages preachers to communicate honestly and directly, ensuring their message is clear and meaningful. At the same time, it reminds them to approach these conversations with a spirit of love and compassion. By following the principles outlined in this verse, preachers—young and old alike—can effectively convey complex messages in a sincere and sensitive way. This makes room for growth and understanding. When preachers tackle challenging subjects, they demonstrate their commitment to guiding and supporting their community through all aspects of life, including the tough and uncomfortable ones. This approach helps the congregation navigate complex issues in the light of spiritual teaching, which will aid in their personal growth.

Additionally, addressing sensitive topics allows for a more comprehensive exploration of the human experience. I'm referring to the importance of delving into the wide range of human emotions, struggles, and pitfalls people encounter. This exploration helps individuals connect their personal experiences with spiritual teaching and also helps them find peace, wisdom, and guidance in the Word of God.

By courageously and boldly addressing these subjects with care, preachers can foster a sense of unity, compassion, and understanding among the listeners, where all members can feel seen, heard, and supported on their spiritual journey.

The Triad

A triad is a group of three key elements that work together harmoniously. It's like having three essential puzzle pieces that fit perfectly together to create a complete picture. Similarly, a triad of essential components plays a key role when delving into challenging subjects. When these elements work together smoothly, tackling difficult or uncomfortable topics becomes manageable for the preacher and a blessing to the hearer. That triad is made up of *grace, humility,* and *biblical wisdom.* Let's take a moment and dive deeper into the specific roles that each of these elements plays.

Grace

Grace is a multi-faceted concept, and in this book, I address it in two distinct ways. First, I want to define grace as *divine assistance.* This refers to the unmerited favor and support we receive from God. This is the grace that empowers us in our weaknesses, gives us strength in moments of need, sustains us throughout our journey of faith, and gives us what we need to operate in our spiritual gifts. It's the supernatural help that allows us to accomplish what we couldn't do on our own.

However, grace also plays a critical role in the way we

communicate, especially when presenting difficult messages. In this context, grace is the ability to convey messages with kindness, empathy, and understanding. This type of grace is about having the wisdom to address sensitive topics in a way that reflects the heart of God, ensuring that we build bridges rather than burn them. It's about extending compassion and love through our words, even when discussing challenging or controversial subjects.

Both dimensions of grace—God's divine assistance and the grace we extend in our communication—are vital for effective ministry. Understanding when and how to apply each one can help us be better vessels of God's truth while maintaining a spirit of love and humility. Without grace, your message may come across as harsh, judgmental, or insensitive, potentially alienating your audience and hindering their ability to connect with the message you're trying to convey. Grace creates a safe and welcoming space for discussions on complex topics, fostering a sense of openness and receptiveness among listeners. Remember that grace isn't about compromising on what's wrong or sinful; it's more about sharing the truth in a loving and compassionate manner.

Additionally, grace has this fantastic way of nurturing empathy, forgiveness, and unity within the congregation. That is what touches the hearts of the listeners. This empathy helps people feel heard and valued, making it easier for them to forgive themselves and move forward. By embracing grace in your preaching, you create a sense of togetherness among the congregation, making a supportive and inclusive community where everyone feels connected and uplifted.

You must recognize that in order to extend grace in your communication you had to have shown kindness and forgiveness to yourself at some point. Even as a preacher, you have not always been perfect, even if the only people who know about your mistakes are God and yourself. The same compassion and empathy you offered to yourself are the same qualities you can share with your audience. By acknowledging your own journey of self-compassion, you can authentically connect with others and create a space where grace and understanding can flow freely.

For instance, you can share your personal stories of struggle and growth to connect with the congregation intimately, showing that everyone faces challenges. Also, using inclusive words, such as *we* instead of *you* or *y'all* promotes unity and respect, showing that no one is above another. This allows for equality and belonging, showing that we are all valued community members regardless of our differences.

Extending grace allows for understanding and truth without judgment or condemnation when discussing sensitive topics. It encourages individuals to approach difficult issues with kindness and patience, giving space for growth within the congregation. By embodying grace in communication, preachers can demonstrate forgiveness and acceptance, promoting togetherness and healing among the audience. Ultimately, grace in preaching serves as a guiding light that illuminates the path toward empathy, forgiveness, and unity, nurturing a supportive and inclusive environment for all.

Humility

Humility plays a significant role in addressing sensitive topics in preaching, as it allows the preacher to approach discussions with a sense of openness and vulnerability. When a preacher demonstrates humility, it shows a willingness to listen, learn, and empathize with the experiences and perspectives of others. Setting aside ego and pride will encourage mutual respect and collaboration, leading to more meaningful conversations and deeper insights into sensitive issues.

Navigating a challenging topic without humility can lead to a lack of understanding and connection with the congregation. Without humility, preachers will present themselves as arrogant or dismissive. The absence of humility can create a barrier between the preacher and the audience, making it challenging to address sensitive issues effectively. It may actually cause division rather than unity within the community. Imagine a preacher approaching a complex topic with a know-it-all attitude, not considering the congregation's experiences. This preacher would be perceived as condescending or self-righteous, making it difficult for the audience to relate to or engage with the message. Without humility, the preacher's communication would lack empathy and understanding, leading to a disconnect between the pulpit and the pew. But by embracing humility as a guiding principle, a minister can approach tough subjects with grace and compassion, leading to a more understanding environment where listening, learning, and growing are possible.

Biblical Wisdom

I must say that biblical wisdom is the most crucial element of the triad. When delving into challenging topics, biblical wisdom holds the foundational insights and principles that will help navigate sensitive issues with grace and understanding. Biblical wisdom makes way for a foundation rooted in timeless truths and teaching, providing a framework for addressing complex matters. By incorporating the Bible, preachers can draw upon the stories and lessons from Scripture to offer guidance, hope, and healing to the congregation in times of uncertainty and difficulty.

The term *biblical wisdom* refers to the divine principles and truths from the Bible that guide a preacher's words and actions when delivering a sermon. We must utilize wisdom, insight, and moral lessons found in Scripture to communicate spiritually enriching messages that are relevant and impactful to the listeners' lives. Communicating these biblical truths helps the wisdom resonate with the hearts and minds of the audience, fostering growth, reflection, and lasting spiritual transformation.

Biblical wisdom should serve as a compass for preachers when addressing challenging issues, shaping their perspectives and responses with divine guidance and moral clarity. Please read that again. We do not force the Bible to fit our preconceived thoughts and opinions. We must shape our thoughts according to the wisdom offered by the Bible. By grounding your perspectives and responses in biblical principles, you can provide valuable insights and solutions for addressing the controversial issue you're communicating about.

Young preachers must rely on biblical wisdom instead of just sharing opinions when discussing complex topics. When we lean on and insert our own opinions, it can lead to misunderstandings and bias. But when we prioritize and approach a topic through the lens of biblical wisdom, we speak from a place of truth and authority. This helps us build trust, credibility, and effective communication within the congregation. The bottom line is: The Bible must be the foundation of everything we say. We must intentionally integrate biblical wisdom throughout our messages.

Biblical wisdom provides a solid foundation for guidance, and it helps preachers navigate sensitive topics with grace, authority, and clarity. By relying on the timeless teachings of the Bible, preachers can effectively address complex subjects, foster understanding, and promote unity within the congregation. Biblical wisdom ensures that the message is grounded in truth and offers a source of inspiration, hope, and transformation for those listening.

Scripture will always be relevant and powerful. It is what helps us maintain a grounded and insightful approach. I encourage you to practice studying and meditating on the scriptures, not just to preach but to give you the biblical wisdom you need to address difficult topics at any time. Navigating difficult topics will become smooth sailing when you utilize the triad of *grace*, *humility*, and *biblical wisdom*.

Let's take the topic of mental health and see how the triad of grace, humility, and biblical wisdom can help a preacher navigate this sensitive subject:

Grace: Start by extending grace through your tone and approach. Acknowledge that the topic may be challenging and that everyone is at a different place in their understanding or experience. For example, when speaking about mental health, you might say something like, "We all have struggles, and it's important to know that God's love does not require or depend on our perfection. He meets us where we are." This creates an atmosphere of compassion, which can open hearts to receive the message.

Humility: Humility is crucial in showing that you, too, are on a journey. Stress that you're not speaking from a place of judgment but from your own ongoing relationship with God. For example, you might share, "I don't have all the answers, and I've wrestled with understanding this issue myself, but I believe God calls us to care for our mental, emotional, and spiritual health." This allows the congregation to see that you are not setting yourself above them but walking alongside them in faith.

Biblical Wisdom: Finally, provide biblical wisdom by grounding your message in Scripture. Instead of relying solely on personal opinions or societal stigmas, you should turn to the Bible for guidance. For a sermon on mental health, you might reference passages like Philippians 4:6 and 7, which encourages us to bring our anxieties to God, or Psalm 34:18, which speaks of God's closeness to the brokenhearted. These verses offer comfort while also directing the congregation to biblical solutions for dealing with their struggles. These teachings also foster empathy, understanding, and support within the congregation.

By weaving these three elements together, you offer a message that not only speaks truth but does so in a way that reflects Christ's love and compassion—all while promoting healing and acceptance among all church community members.

The Risks

When addressing complex topics, it's important to understand that risks are involved. So imagine this scenario: You're standing in front of your congregation, about to dive into a sermon that tackles a controversial issue head-on. You might feel a mix of excitement and apprehension. Why? Because you know that addressing these topics can come with challenges. It's like walking a fine line, where you must balance truth and the potential for negative reactions or division.

However, you can acknowledge these risks from the start and allow yourself the opportunity to approach these conversations with wisdom, grace, and a deep understanding of the complexities involved. For this reason, it is necessary to explore how we can navigate these challenges and create a space where empathy can thrive within our congregation.

When addressing controversial topics in sermons, preachers may face several challenges. One of the main challenges is navigating differing opinions within the congregation. People have diverse backgrounds, beliefs, and life experiences, which can lead to conflicting viewpoints on sensitive subjects. As a preacher, it's your responsibility to approach these topics with sensitivity and respect for the diversity of perspectives.

Emotional reactions are another challenge that can arise when discussing controversial topics. People may have strong feelings or personal connections to specific issues, and these emotions can sometimes cloud their ability to engage with the message. As a preacher, you should create a safe and inclusive space where individuals feel comfortable expressing their emotions while encouraging respectful and thoughtful conversations.

Potential conflicts can also emerge when addressing controversial topics. Disagreements and tensions may arise between individuals or groups within the congregation. Be mindful of these potential conflicts and make every effort to foster an environment of understanding and reconciliation. This can be done through promoting active listening, encouraging empathy, and emphasizing the importance of respectful dialogue.

Another risk is the potential for division within the congregation. A preacher's role is to promote unity, not division. By embracing grace, you create a harmonious and united community. But as we've previously stated, controversial topics can bring about strong reactions and differing opinions among church members. If not handled carefully, this can lead to divisions and more conflicts.

It would be best if you were prepared for backlash from individuals. It's possible that some people may strongly disagree with your stance to the point where they resort to criticism or even personal attacks. In addition to that, you should also prepare for possible loss of trust. Addressing controversial topics, if not handled properly, may result in the people no longer trusting your voice and authority. You can avoid this by always leaving room for respect and understanding between the people and the preacher.

Something else to consider is the impact on the reputation of the church. Controversial sermons or statements can have an effect on the reputation of the church within the larger community, and negative publicity or misinterpretation of the preacher's message may lead to a tarnished image or even a decrease in attendance. Considering this risk and other potential consequences before addressing controversial issues is a necessary step to take.

You should always approach these topics with wisdom and discernment. By emphasizing the importance of always making unity the goal, preachers can create a space where understanding thrives.

This will create an atmosphere where everyone feels valued and included while hearing the truth of the Word of God, even when discussing challenging subjects.

Practical Strategies

When navigating controversial topics, as a young preacher, you can benefit from several practical strategies.

Here are some steps to consider:

1. Thorough Research: Take the time to gather information from reliable sources. This will help you comprehensively understand different perspectives, historical context, and relevant Bible truths.
2. Begin by setting aside time for focused prayer, asking God for wisdom and clarity as you prepare to address difficult topics. Practical steps might include praying, "God, guide my words and help me speak with truth and compassion," or "Lord, give me insight into the needs of my congregation." Journaling any insights or scriptures that come to mind during prayer can provide direction for your sermon. This practice helps align your message with God's will and offers clarity as you navigate complex issues.
3. Seek Wise Counsel: Reach out to trusted mentors and colleagues who are experts on the subject you're exploring. Their insights and advice can help you navigate potential challenges and determine the best action.

Adopting these strategies allows you to navigate controversial topics thoughtfully and promote unity within the congregation. Remember to approach these discussions with grace, humility, and biblical wisdom, focusing on fostering understanding among your listeners and communicating truth in a loving way.

I want to emphasize the importance of using respectful and inclusive language when discussing sensitive issues. If we resort to derogatory phrases or offensive language, we create barriers instead of fostering understanding. Language like that can alienate and offend people, hindering their ability to engage in meaningful dialogue and gain a deeper understanding of the topic.

By choosing our words carefully and respecting others, we create an environment where transformation and truth can abide. When we approach discussions gracefully, we open the door for constructive conversations that promote unity and bridge gaps of misunderstanding. It's about recognizing the power of our words and using them to build bridges rather than walls.

The Need for Boldness

When tackling difficult subjects and understanding the tools and risks involved, there's yet one element we must have to navigate complex topics successfully: boldness.

Boldness in addressing sensitive issues allows us to speak with conviction, confidence, and clarity. It empowers us to tackle challenging subjects head-on, even when there may be resistance or discomfort. Let's explore ways that you, as a young preacher, can cultivate and express boldness in your sermons and discussions.

First and foremost, young preachers must have a deep understanding of the topic at hand. Thorough research, study, and reflection create a solid foundation of knowledge. This knowledge equips you with the confidence to speak boldly and authoritatively, knowing you have done your due diligence. By immersing yourself in the subject matter, you can articulate your thoughts with clarity and conviction, making a compelling case for your message.

Another aspect of possessing boldness is the willingness to challenge the status quo. This requires stepping outside of your comfort zone and addressing topics that may be considered controversial or unpopular. This doesn't mean intentionally provoking conflict but instead having the courage to address issues that must be discussed within the congregation. You can foster boldness within yourself by embracing your role as a spiritual leader and understanding that your duty extends beyond delivering sermons that merely make congregation members feel comfortable. By speaking truthfully and fearlessly, you can inspire change, growth, and transformation within your community.

Furthermore, boldness can be expressed through personal examples. Sharing personal experiences and connecting them to the topic at hand allows you to speak from a place of authenticity and vulnerability. By sharing your struggles, doubts, and triumphs, you create a relatable and engaging sermon that resonates with the congregation. This genuine approach showcases your boldness and encourages openness and vulnerability among the listeners.

Deepening your knowledge, challenging the status quo, and sharing personal anecdotes can help you speak with conviction, confidence, and clarity. Boldness also enables you to inspire change and growth within the congregation. So I encourage you to embrace your role as a bold spiritual leader and defender, fearlessly sharing the truth and fostering a community of openness and transformation.

To sum it all up, preachers should always approach controversial issues with humility, grace, and a commitment to seeking truth and unity within the church community. It would be best to strive to be clear and confident in your message while being empathetic and understanding toward others. Embracing the concept of grace means promoting forgiveness and empathy among the congregation. Preachers should also navigate sensitive topics with wisdom, discernment, and a focus on fostering unity. Doing so can create an environment where everyone feels heard and valued.

Young preacher, you can make a difference by using respectful language, practicing empathy, seeking truth, and embodying grace. These principles enhance your ability to create an inclusive environment for growth and change within the congregation. Give the truth boldly. Give the truth compassionately.

— 99 —

BIBLICAL
WISDOM SHOULD SERVE AS A COMPASS FOR PREACHERS WHEN ADDRESSING CHALLENGING ISSUES, SHAPING THEIR PERSPECTIVES AND RESPONSES WITH DIVINE GUIDANCE AND MORAL CLARITY.

— 99 —

Chapter 6

Leading Worship

Worship is the heartbeat of the church—a sacred space where believers unite to honor God and deepen their connection with Him and one another. It goes beyond just tradition; worship includes various expressions, from uplifting music and heartfelt prayer to the shared reading of Scripture and hearing of the message. In these moments, the church fulfills its divine purpose, glorifying God, nurturing spiritual growth, and cultivating a strong sense of community among its members.

At its core, worship responds to God's love, grace, and goodness. It is a way for individuals and the church as a whole to express gratitude, awe, and reverence for God. Through worship, believers acknowledge God's sovereignty and His role as the Creator and Sustainer of all things. It is a time to reflect on God's attributes, such as love, mercy, and faithfulness.

Worship also serves as a means of spiritual nourishment and growth. It is a time for believers to engage with God's Word through Scripture readings and the sermon. The teaching and preaching during worship services provide guidance, encouragement, and instruction for living out the Christian faith. It is an opportunity for believers to deepen their understanding of God's truth and apply it to their lives.

Additionally, worship helps foster community within the church. It is a time for believers to unite in their faith, to worship and serve God as one body. Through worship, believers experience a sense of belonging, support, and encouragement. It is a time to share in the joys and sorrows of fellow believers, pray for one another, and build relationships beyond the church walls.

Furthermore, worship has the power to transform lives. It is when individuals can encounter God's presence, experience His love, and be transformed by His grace. It is a time when believers can find and experience healing, hope, and restoration. Worship provides a space for individuals to lay their burdens down, seek forgiveness, and experience freedom that comes from surrendering to God.

As you can see, the significance of worship in the church is multifaceted. It is a time of reverence, gratitude, and connection with God. It is a means of spiritual growth, a source of community and support, and a transformative encounter with the divine. Worship is an integral part of the identity and mission of the church, shaping the lives of believers and drawing them closer to God and to one another.

As the preacher, you have a unique role in leading the people through worship. You become the guide, facilitator, and leader who helps the congregation engage with God in a meaningful way. Through your words, presence, and actions, you set the tone for the worship experience and create an atmosphere where people can connect with God.

Psalm 100:2 says, "Worship the Lord with gladness; come before him with joyful songs." This shows the importance of approaching worship with a cheerful and grateful heart. As the preacher and leader of worship, you act as the forerunner of the congregation's worship experience. By encouraging them to worship the Lord with gladness and to come before Him with joyful hearts, you can help create an atmosphere of celebration and gratitude.

Keep in mind that worship is not just a duty or obligation but a joyful response to God's goodness and faithfulness. It reminds us to approach worship with thanksgiving and praise, recognizing that God deserves our wholehearted devotion. As you lead the congregation through the time of worship, you can draw their attention to God's goodness, inviting them to join in the various expressions of worship.

Understanding Worship

Worship is a central aspect of the Christian faith. It encompasses a variety of elements that come together to honor and glorify God. Every aspect is purposed to deepen our relationship with God as we acknowledge Him and seek His presence. Through worship, we can draw closer to God, experience His peace and joy, and align our hearts and minds with His will.

I want to emphasize that worship incorporates various elements that enhance our connection with God. It's not just about a slow-tempo song that we are cultured to lift our hands to. On the contrary, there are a variety of components that come together to create a meaningful encounter with God.

Prayer is vital to worship. It allows us to communicate with God, pour out our hearts, and seek His guidance and provision. It is a way to express our dependence on Him and bring our concerns, praises, and thanksgiving before Him.

Music is another powerful element of worship. It enables us to express our adoration, reverence, and gratitude to God through songs and hymns. Music uniquely touches our hearts, engages our emotions, and lifts our spirits as we join together in collective praise.

Scripture plays a fundamental role in worship as well. It serves as a guide, providing us with God's Word and teachings. Reading and meditating on Scripture during worship helps us better understand God's character, promises, and will for our lives. It allows us to reflect on His truth and apply it to our daily walk with Him.

Lastly, the sermon is an essential part of worship. It is a time when the preacher shares a message from the Bible, providing the congregation with insight, encouragement, and guidance. The sermon helps us grow in our understanding of Scripture and challenges us to live out our faith in practical ways.

By incorporating prayer, music, Scripture, and the sermon, worship becomes a holistic experience that engages our hearts, minds, and spirits. It creates an atmosphere where we can encounter God's presence, receive His truth, and respond in reverence, awe, and gratitude.

Overall, worship is a vital part of the Christian faith that allows believers to connect with God, express their love and devotion to Him, and grow in their relationship with Him. It is a way to honor and glorify God, encompassing various elements that enhance our worship experience.

Creating a Worship Flow

Worship flow is all about carefully planning and arranging the different elements of a worship service to create a smooth and meaningful experience for the congregation. When the worship flow is well-crafted, it helps engage the congregation and allows them to connect more deeply with God and each other. By thoughtfully considering the order and transitions between elements such as music, prayers, Scripture readings, and the sermon, the worship service can flow smoothly and impact the congregation's experience.

A good worship flow builds anticipation and sets the tone for the service. It creates moments for reflection and response, providing intentional spaces for the congregation to engage with God through prayer, the Word, and personal reflection. This helps individuals connect with the message and internalize its meaning personally.

Additionally, a worship flow takes into account the emotional journey of the congregation. It balances moments of joy, celebration, and praise with introspection, confession, and repentance. This variety of emotions creates a holistic worship experience where individuals can express their full range of feelings and experiences in the presence of God.

Seamless integration of different elements is also essential in worship flow. Smooth transitions between music, prayers, Scripture readings, and sermons help maintain the congregation's focus and prevent disruptions or distractions that could hinder their level of engagement.

The impact of the worship flow extends beyond the duration of the service. A well-designed worship flow can leave a lasting impression on the hearts and minds of the congregation. It can create moments of spiritual breakthrough, where individuals encounter God in a profound and transformative way. It fosters an atmosphere of unity, where everyone is connected in their shared worship experience.

Ultimately, worship flow is about intentionally planning and arranging the elements of a worship service to create a seamless and meaningful experience for the congregation.

Here are some practical tips to help you create a dynamic and worship flow that is impactful from the moment you receive the microphone to the time you relinquish your stand:

1. Start with an *opening moment*: This can include a call to worship, an opening prayer to set the tone for the worship, or something as simple as a welcome.
2. Incorporate *different elements*: To keep the worship service engaging and diverse, incorporate a mix of songs, prayers, Scripture readings, testimonies, and congregational participation.
3. Know your *transitions*: Pay attention to the flow between each element. Smooth transitions help maintain the congregation's focus and create a seamless worship experience.
4. Allow for *reflection and response*: This will provide space for the congregation to do a self-analysis to promote lasting change and transformation.
5. Consider the *journey*: Balance moments of joy, celebration, and praise with moments of introspection, confessions, and repentance.
6. Keep the congregation *engaged*: This can include encouraging participation through singing or some other interactive activity during the worship, even if it's something as simple as, "Look at your neighbor and tell them…"
7. End with a *closing moment*: This can be a benediction, a final song, or a time of prayer, leaving the congregation with a sense of peace, encouragement, and inspiration.

Remember, these are just some practical tips to help structure a worship service. Feel free to adapt and customize them based on the needs and preferences of the congregation you're ministering to. The key is to always create a worship experience that is meaningful, engaging, and creates a deep connection with God.

The Sermon and Worship

The preacher's role in integrating the sermon within the worship service is of utmost importance. Why? Because this portion of worship serves as the key opportunity for the preacher to share God's Word and communicate its relevance to the listeners. It's a time when the preacher can delve into Scripture, provide guidance, and offer insights that inspire and challenge the congregation in their faith journey. The sermon helps deepen the understanding of God's teachings, encourages personal reflection, and guides individuals in applying biblical principles to their lives.

You might think, "How does simply listening to a sermon become a part of worship?" It's a time when we actively engage with God's Word, listen attentively, and open our hearts to receive spiritual nourishment and guidance. The sermon invites us to reflect on our relationship with God, challenges us to grow in our faith, and encourages us to live out our beliefs in our daily lives. It propels us into a greater level of worship—not the act but the lifestyle. So by listening to the sermon, we participate in worship to deepen our understanding of God's truth and align our lives with His teachings for our life of worship.

Preachers must understand this because it helps them fulfill their role effectively. By recognizing the impact of their words, preachers can strive to deliver messages that engage, inspire, and connect with the congregation. Understanding that the sermon is a vital part of worship encourages preachers to prepare thoughtfully, study the Scriptures diligently, and seek the guidance of the Holy Spirit in delivering messages that resonate with the hearts of the listeners. Ultimately, recognizing the importance of the sermon in worship empowers preachers to fulfill their responsibility of shepherding and guiding the congregation in their faith journey.

Remember that there are times during worship when the Holy Spirit moves in such a powerful way that it takes over the entire service. It's like in Second Chronicles 5:14 when the glory of the Lord filled the temple, and the priests couldn't even continue with their duties. Witnessing the Spirit's presence at work among the congregation in those moments is incredible. Even if there isn't an opportunity to give a sermon, those moments of divine encounter and spiritual awakening can have a profound impact on everyone present. It reminds us that worship is not just about our plans and programs but about surrendering to God's leading and allowing His Spirit to move in our midst.

Just because there are moments when the Holy Spirit takes over, and the preacher may not have the opportunity to give a sermon, it doesn't mean the preacher shouldn't come prepared. In fact, being prepared shows respect for the congregation and honors the responsibility of sharing God's Word. While the Spirit may lead the service in unexpected ways, the preacher's preparation allows them to be ready to deliver a message when the opportunity arises. It's about balancing being open to the leading of the Spirit and being diligent in study and preparation. So even when the Spirit moves in extraordinary ways, the preacher's preparation can still be vital in facilitating a meaningful worship experience.

Engaging the Congregation

As the leader of the worship experience, you must remember that it's not about you shining as a solo performer , it is about creating a meaningful corporate experience for everyone involved. Instead of hogging the spotlight, focus on facilitating an atmosphere where the congregation feels included and engaged. By shifting the focus from yourself to the congregation and the collective worship experience, you create a space where everyone can connect with God and each other in a meaningful way.

In a corporate worship setting, where our ultimate goal is to glorify the one true and living God, the preacher should always aim to actively engage the congregation. As the leader, the preacher should be facilitating a meaningful worship experience. By connecting with the congregation, the preacher can create an atmosphere of harmony where everyone can collectively lift their voices and hearts in praise to God.

When a preacher fails to engage the congregation in the worship service, it can have negative effects. First, it can lead to disinterest, boredom, and distraction among the congregation. Second, the individual personal development of congregation members can be stunted or slowed. Engagement is needed to ensure spiritual growth. Engaging sermons have the potential to challenge and inspire individuals on their spiritual journey. Finally, a lack of engagement can lead to decreased participation and a weaker sense of community within the church. When individuals don't feel connected or inspired, they may become passive observers instead of active participants.

In short, a preacher who fails to engage a congregation can end up with a church that has a severe lack of connection, limited spiritual growth, and a diminished sense of community among its members. Preachers must actively engage their congregations to create a vibrant and meaningful worship experience.

A preacher who engages the congregation during the worship service connects the preacher and the listeners. This connection allows the congregation to feel seen, heard, and understood. Secondly, an engaged congregation is more likely to be attentive and focused, allowing them to absorb and apply the teachings to their lives. This can lead to personal growth and transformation within the individuals. Lastly, a preacher who successfully engages the congregation can inspire a sense of community. When people feel connected to one another through shared worship experiences, it strengthens the bonds within the church and fosters a supportive and uplifting environment.

There are several ways to engage a congregation during a worship service. One effective way is through interactive elements, such as asking questions or encouraging participation. This can involve inviting the congregation to respond through hand claps, lifted hands, or other methods. Another way is through storytelling and relatable examples that connect with people's lives, as we've seen in previous chapters. Sharing personal experiences or using relatable stories can help the congregation feel engaged and connected to the message. Additionally, incorporating multimedia elements such as videos, visuals, or music can enhance engagement by appealing to different senses and creating a dynamic worship experience. These are just a few ideas, but the key is to create opportunities for active involvement and meaningful connection with the congregation.

The preacher plays an essential role in leading worship services. The preacher guides the congregation's spiritual journey, delivers the message, and facilitates a meaningful worship experience.

I encourage you to approach your ministry with authenticity, passion, and a heart for facilitating meaningful worship experiences by setting an example yourself. By being genuine in your call for worship, you can inspire others to do the same. Passion is contagious, so when leading the worship, you can demonstrate enthusiasm for the message and the worship service, which can inspire others to engage and participate. Having a heart for facilitating meaningful worship experiences means prioritizing the needs and spiritual growth of the congregation. Put your focus on creating an inclusive and welcoming environment, incorporating interactive elements, and being open to feedback and suggestions from the congregation. You can inspire others and create impactful worship experiences by embodying these qualities.

— 99 —

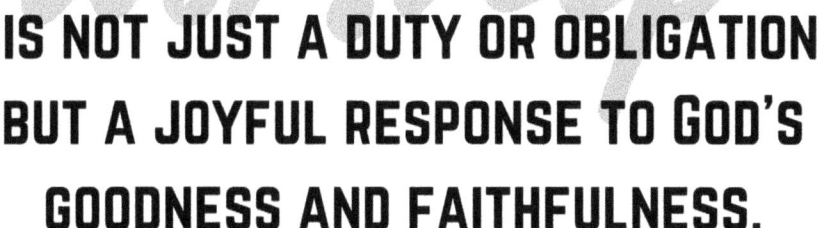

IS NOT JUST A DUTY OR OBLIGATION
BUT A JOYFUL RESPONSE TO GOD'S
GOODNESS AND FAITHFULNESS.

— 99 —

Chapter 7

Cultivating Authenticity

We must dive deeper into the topic of authenticity than we did in the first chapter of this manual. Let's uncover its significance together.

In Galatians 1:10, the apostle Paul wrote, "Am I now trying to win the approval of human beings, or of God? Or am I trying to please people? If I were still trying to please people, I would not be a servant of Christ." This verse reminds us of the importance of staying true to our convictions and being authentic in our preaching. It encourages us to prioritize pleasing God over seeking the approval of others. By cultivating authenticity, we can focus on delivering God's message with sincerity and integrity rather than conforming to the expectations of others. This verse reminds us to embrace our identity as servants of Christ and to let that guide our preaching. This allows us to have a genuine and meaningful impact on the lives of others.

When it comes to preaching, the expectations of others can sometimes create a prison that hinders our authenticity. People may have specific ideas or standards of what a preacher should be like or how he or she should deliver a message. These expectations can pressure us to conform to a particular style or content, even if it doesn't align with our true selves. However, genuine authenticity in preaching comes from speaking from the heart, sharing personal experiences, and allowing a message to flow naturally.

When we let go of the expectations and embrace our authentic voice, we can connect with our congregation on a deeper level. So let's break free from the prison of expectations and preach in a way that reflects our true selves and the message we feel called to share. This is what cultivating authenticity is all about.

Cultivating our authenticity in preaching allows us to connect with our congregation more deeply. Our messages become more relatable and impactful when we're genuine to ourselves. People can sense when we're being authentic, creating an atmosphere of trust and openness. By sharing our struggles, doubts, and triumphs, we show that we're human too, which helps our congregation feel comfortable sharing their experiences. Authentic preaching also allows the Holy Spirit to work through us, guiding our words and touching the hearts of those who listen. It breaks down barriers and encourages a sense of community, where everyone feels safe to be themselves.

Genuine and Transparent Preaching

When cultivating authenticity in preaching, genuine and transparent preaching holds immense significance. Through genuine and transparent preaching, we can connect with our congregation and deliver messages that resonate with their hearts and souls.

Authenticity in preaching means being true to ourselves, embracing our unique voice, and sharing our personal experiences and stories. When we preach authentically, we create an environment that allows our congregation to feel comfortable and engaged. By being genuine and transparent, we show our vulnerability and humanity, which can be incredibly powerful in connecting with others. When we share our own struggles, doubts, and triumphs, we invite our congregation to do the same. Authentic preaching also encourages a deeper level of connection with God. When we are true to ourselves, we allow God's power to work through us. In this authenticity, we can effectively convey God's love, grace, and truth to our congregation.

Furthermore, genuine and transparent preaching helps break down barriers and eliminates the perception of a "perfect" preacher. It reminds us that we are all on a faith journey, learning and growing together. When we share our struggles and doubts, we create a safe space for others to do the same, fostering an environment of authenticity and growth.

By understanding who we are and what we stand for, we can develop a preaching style that is true to ourselves. This involves embracing our strengths and weaknesses, being open to feedback, and continually growing in faith and understanding.

Ultimately, genuine and transparent preaching allows us to be vessels of God's message, delivering it with sincerity, integrity, and love. It enables us to connect more deeply with our congregation, inspiring and encouraging them in their faith journeys.

The Power of Authenticity

Regarding preaching, it's important to have authenticity at the core. Without it, genuine and transparent preaching becomes challenging. When a preacher is authentic, his or her words carry more weight and impact. It creates a space where the congregation can find themselves in the message and feel a genuine connection. Authenticity and the anointing of God are major keys to powerful and impactful preaching.

The opposite of being authentic in preaching is not meaning what you say—*in*authenticity. Someone might preach or act in a way that doesn't match his or her true morals and convictions. This could involve preaching for personal gain or attempting to deceive others. On the other hand, being authentic in preaching means being genuine, sincere, and true to yourself, to the message, and yielding to the guidance of the Holy Spirit. It's about being genuine and honest in what you preach.

When someone preaches without authenticity, it can have some negative consequences. First, people can sense when a preacher is not being genuine, and it can create a disconnect between the preacher and the listeners. Additionally, it can undermine the preacher's credibility and trustworthiness. If someone merely says words they genuinely don't live by, it can be perceived as lacking depth and substance. Ultimately, preaching without authenticity can hinder the impact and effectiveness of the message, as it lacks the genuine connection and sincerity that comes from being true to oneself.

Remember that authenticity in preaching isn't about relying solely on our abilities but instead placing our trust in the Holy Spirit to work through us. It's about surrendering our gifts and talents to Him, allowing Him to shape and use them for His purposes. When we trust the Holy Spirit with our abilities, we open ourselves to His guidance, wisdom, and power. This trust marks genuine authenticity because it acknowledges that our effectiveness as preachers comes from God's work in and through us rather than our efforts alone. It's a beautiful partnership between our willingness and the Spirit's leading, resulting in a genuine preaching experience. When we embrace this trust in the Holy Spirit, we can genuinely embody authenticity in our preaching.

Our experiences can influence authenticity, and sometimes those experiences can lead us away from who God intended us to be. Allowing our negative experiences or hardships to shape us in a way that contradicts God's plan for our lives can taint our authenticity. For example, if we've been hurt or betrayed, we may develop a guarded or hateful demeanor that doesn't reflect the love and grace that God desires for us to show to others. It's important to remember that authenticity is not about letting our experiences define us but allowing God to shape and transform us into who He intended us to be.

That's what being yourself is about—being the YOU that God made. By seeking His guidance, relying on His Word, and staying connected to Him through prayer and worship, we can ensure that our authenticity aligns with His will for our lives.

That is why the power of authenticity truly comes from discovering our identity in God rather than solely pursuing what our fleshly desires may crave. It's about seeking God's will and aligning our desires with His plans. When we focus on becoming who God created us to be, we tap into a more profound sense of purpose and fulfillment. It's not about chasing temporary pleasures or worldly ambitions like honorariums and gigs but about finding our true identity and living by God's truth. By seeking to understand who we are in God, we unlock the power of authenticity and live a life that reflects His love and grace.

Strategies To Cultivate Authenticity
Strategy 1

Align your beliefs with your actions. By this, I mean that as a preacher, you cultivate authenticity when you "practice what you preach." So when we say live out the teachings you preach, it's not just about "talking the talk" but also about "walking the walk." When you show through your actions and behavior that you genuinely believe in what you preach, it dramatically impacts others.

To make it more understandable, imagine you're telling your friends to always be kind and respectful to others. But if they see you being mean or disrespectful, they won't take your words seriously. It's essential to be a good example by treating others with kindness and respect, just like you tell them to do.

Another vital aspect is integrating these teachings into your daily life. It's not just about preaching on certain days but about applying these teachings in practical ways every day. For example, if you're talking about forgiveness, show how forgiveness can positively impact your relationships and how you practice forgiveness in your own life.

Consistency is also crucial. This means you need to be the same person both in public and in private. Your words should match your actions, and people should see that you genuinely believe in your preaching. It helps build trust and authenticity.

Lastly, practicing what you preach means actively participating in the practices and rituals of your faith. Doing so will deepen your connection with the teachings and set an example for others. Through this, you build consistency between your words and your lifestyle. This consistency helps create trust and credibility with your congregation. It's about living out the values and principles you teach so that your words and lifestyle are harmonious. Doing so makes you a genuine and authentic example for others to follow.

Strategy 2

Be transparent with the congregation. Opening up about personal struggles and vulnerabilities is a powerful way to cultivate authenticity in preaching. When you share your challenges and vulnerabilities, your congregation will see you're human just like them. This creates a sense of relatability and empathy.

One way to expand on this is by sharing personal stories that connect with your message. For example, if you're preaching about overcoming fear, you could share a story about facing and overcoming fear with your faith's help. By sharing these experiences, you show that you understand what it's like to go through difficult times and how to be guided by your faith.

It's important to remember that sharing personal struggles

doesn't mean you have to reveal every intimate detail of your life. Be discerning and share what you feel comfortable with and what will serve the purpose of the message. The goal is to create an atmosphere where people feel safe to share their struggles.

Additionally, sharing vulnerabilities allows others to see that you're not perfect and that you too, must rely on God's grace. It breaks down the walls of perfectionism and encourages others to embrace their imperfections. This vulnerability can deepen the connection between you and your congregation.

Opening up about your challenges creates a safe space for others to do the same. This vulnerability builds trust and strengthens the bond between you and your congregation, allowing the message to resonate deeper. Being transparent and authentic creates an environment where people feel understood, supported, and inspired to grow in their faith.

Strategy 3

Embrace the guidance of the Holy Spirit. Embracing the guidance of the Holy Spirit means surrendering to God's wisdom and direction. It's about letting go of our plans and desires and allowing the Holy Spirit to lead us in our preaching. By surrendering, we acknowledge that God's wisdom surpasses our own and that we must ultimately follow His direction. It's a beautiful act of trust and faith as we open ourselves up to being vessels for the Holy Spirit's message. Surrendering to God's wisdom and embracing the guidance of the Holy Spirit brings authenticity to our preaching as we rely on His divine guidance rather than solely on our understanding. It invites others to do the same and experience the Holy Spirit's transformative power.

Allowing the Holy Spirit to shape your message is paramount in preaching. When we surrender to the Holy Spirit's guidance, we open ourselves to divine inspiration and wisdom. The Holy Spirit knows the congregation's needs and can speak directly to their hearts. By allowing the Holy Spirit to shape our message, we ensure that it is aligned with God's truth and tailored to the specific needs of those listening. It brings a sense of authenticity and power to our preaching as we become conduits for the Holy Spirit's transformative work.

When we yield to the Holy Spirit, we invite His presence and anointing, making our message impactful and life changing.

It's important to note that allowing the Holy Spirit to shape your message doesn't mean you sit back and do nothing. It's a partnership between you and the Holy Spirit. You still put in the effort to study and prepare, but you do so with an open heart and a willingness to be led. As you do this, you tap into a divine source of wisdom and inspiration.

Embracing the guidance of the Holy Spirit brings wisdom, power, and anointing to our words, enabling us to communicate God's truth effectively. By relying on the Holy Spirit, we acknowledge our dependence on God and create an atmosphere of humility and spiritual impact.

Strategy 4

Continuously reflect and grow. One way to do this is by regularly examining and being honest about your motives and intentions. Now and then, it's necessary to take a step back and reflect on why you do what you do. Ask yourself questions like:

- Why am I passionate about sharing the message of God?
- Am I seeking to glorify God or myself through my preaching?
- Are my intentions focused on helping others grow in their faith?
- Is my preaching motivated by a genuine desire to bring people closer to God?

Doing this ensures that your actions align with your values and that you're true to yourself. This is a great way to cultivate self-awareness and continue on the path of personal growth and authenticity.

Being open to feedback and constructive criticism allows us to gain valuable insights and perspectives we may have yet to consider. It helps us identify blind spots, areas for improvement, and growth opportunities. By receiving feedback with an open mind, we can refine our beliefs, actions, and preaching style, ensuring that we are constantly evolving and staying true to our purpose. Embracing feedback also demonstrates humility and a willingness to learn, which fosters trust and connection with the congregation. Ultimately, being open to feedback empowers us to become more authentic, effective, and impactful in our preaching journey. We'll discuss that more in the next chapter.

Overcoming the Challenges

There are several reasons a preacher may experience fears and insecurities in preaching authentically. Sometimes, it stems from a fear of judgment or criticism from the congregation. We may worry about not being good enough or fear our message won't resonate with others. Additionally, the responsibility of delivering a message from God can create feelings of inadequacy or imposter syndrome. We may question our knowledge, experience, or ability to convey the truth effectively. These fears and insecurities are natural and common among preachers because we deeply care about our calling and want to impact others positively. However, by acknowledging and addressing these fears, we can grow and cultivate a more profound sense of authenticity in our preaching.

Addressing fears and insecurities in preaching authentically can be challenging but transformative. It's natural to have concerns and doubts about ourselves and our abilities, but acknowledging and addressing these fears can cultivate a more profound sense of authenticity in our preaching.

Here are some ways you can navigate and overcome these challenges:

1. **Recognize That It's Normal**: First, acknowledge that feeling insecure is a normal part of the preaching journey. It shows that you care deeply about your calling and want to make a difference. Feeling nervous or unsure is okay, but don't let those feelings hold you back from sharing your message.

2. **Embrace Your Unique Voice**: Remember, there's only one you! Embrace your unique voice, personality, and style of preaching. Don't try to imitate others or be someone you're not. Your authenticity shines through when you're true to yourself. Trust in the grace of God on the gifts and talents that God has given you.

3. **Prepare and Practice**: Take the time to study and understand

the Scriptures, the message you want to convey, and the needs of your congregation. The more you prepare, the more confident you'll feel when delivering your sermon. Practice in front of a mirror or with a trusted friend to gain even more confidence.

4. **Address Your Insecurities Head-on**: You must confront your fears and insecurities directly. Take some time for self-reflection and identify what precisely makes you feel insecure. Is it a fear of judgment, criticism, or not being good enough? Once you pinpoint the root cause, challenge those negative thoughts and replace them with positive affirmations. Remind yourself of your purpose and the impact you can make.

5. **Seek Support and Mentorship**: Be bold and reach out for support. Connect with other preachers, mentors, or congregation members who can provide guidance and encouragement. Surround yourself with a community that uplifts and supports you. Remember, we're all in this together!

6. **Pray for Guidance**: Turn to God in prayer. Seek His guidance and ask the Holy Spirit to work through you as you prepare and deliver your sermons. Trust that God has called you for a purpose and will equip you with what you need.

Authenticity allows the message to resonate deeply with the congregation. When you're authentic, you're being genuine and true to who God wants you to be, which creates a connection with your listeners. As discussed earlier in this manual, I encourage you to embrace your unique personalities, styles, and voices. Remember that God created us uniquely and wants to use our individuality to impact lives. Authenticity invites people to see the real you and experience the power of God's truth through your words.

Know that authenticity doesn't mean perfection. It's about being transparent and honest about your journey and struggles. Doing so creates a safe space for others to share their struggles and find hope. Young preacher, your authenticity will inspire others to seek a deeper relationship with God and find comfort in knowing they're not alone in their challenges.

Also, remember to cultivate authenticity by aligning your beliefs with your actions. It's not just about what you say from the pulpit but also how you live your life day to day. Strive for integrity and consistency in your words, actions, and character. People are looking for genuine examples of faith, which is a powerful testimony when it is witnessed in the life of a person living authentically. Your impact extends far beyond the sermon itself.

Lastly, always allow the Holy Spirit to guide your message. Spend time in prayer and seek the Holy Spirit's guidance before, during, and after your sermons. When you rely on the Spirit's leading, your authenticity will be infused with divine power and wisdom. It's not about your abilities but about surrendering to God's work through you. Your impact will be far more significant when you let the Holy Spirit lead.

Remember, authenticity is a journey, and it's something that you can continually cultivate throughout your ministry. By reinforcing its importance and embracing who God wants you to be, you can make a lasting impact on the lives of those you serve by authentically being you.

— 99 —

...AUTHENTICITY IS NOT ABOUT LETTING OUR EXPERIENCES DEFINE US BUT ALLOWING GOD TO SHAPE AND TRANSFORM US INTO WHO HE INTENDED US TO BE.

— 99 —

Chapter 8

Handling Feedback

As a young preacher, you must prioritize embracing a growth mindset. Cultivating a mentality that encourages continuous learning, improvement, and adaptability will enhance your preaching journey. By adopting a growth mindset, you can better face challenges, actively seek feedback, and develop your skills to become a more effective and impactful communicator of the truth. This mindset lays the foundation for your personal and professional growth, reinforcing your belief in your ability to learn, improve, and overcome obstacles along the way.

When you adopt a growth mindset, you understand that your abilities and skills are not fixed but can be developed through dedication and effort. This mindset empowers you to view setbacks and failures as opportunities for learning and growth rather than as indications of your limitations or worth.

With a growth mindset, you become more resilient and persistent in your pursuit of excellence. You become more willing to take on new challenges, step out of your comfort zone, and embrace constructive feedback. You understand that your current abilities are just a starting point and that with consistent effort and deliberate practice, you can continually enhance your preaching skills and deepen your understanding of the truth.

Moreover, cultivating a growth mindset fosters a sense of curiosity and a passion for lifelong learning in your preaching journey. As a young preacher with this mindset, you will be open to new ideas, perspectives, and approaches to preaching. Actively seeking opportunities to expand your knowledge, engaging with diverse theological concepts, and exploring various preaching styles will enable you to connect with a broader range of congregations and communicate the truth in ways that resonate with your listeners.

Additionally, embracing a growth mindset encourages you to

collaborate and seek mentorship, further enhancing your development as a preacher. You recognize the value of learning from others with more experience and wisdom in preaching. By seeking guidance and feedback from seasoned preachers, you can gain valuable insights, refine your skills, and avoid common pitfalls.

Ultimately, embracing a growth mindset empowers you to reach your full potential and make a lasting impact in your congregations and communities. It allows you to continuously evolve, adapt, and refine your preaching style, ensuring your messages remain relevant, authentic, and impactful.

Proverbs 12:1 states, "Whoever loves discipline loves knowledge, but whoever hates correction is stupid." This powerful verse speaks to the importance of young preachers knowing how to handle feedback well. It emphasizes the value of embracing correction and viewing it as an opportunity for growth and learning. When young preachers approach feedback with an open mind and a willingness to learn, they can cultivate a growth mindset and continue to develop in their ministry.

Proverbs 12:1 also highlights the significance of loving discipline and knowledge in conjunction with feedback. Young preachers who love discipline understand that feedback is meant to help them grow and become better preachers. They recognize that receiving feedback indicates that others care about their development and want to see them succeed. By actively seeking knowledge through feedback, they can enhance their preaching skills and connect more deeply with their congregation.

On the other hand, those who resist or reject feedback hinder their own growth and limit their own potential as preachers. Proverbs 12:1 reminds young preachers that refusing correction is not beneficial and can hinder their progress. Remember, feedback is a valuable resource for growth and development. Embrace it with an open mind and a love for knowledge, and you'll continue to grow as a preacher.

Creating a Safe Environment

To thrive in your journey as a young preacher, you need a sanctuary—a safe and non-judgmental space where you can openly receive feedback and gain insights from diverse perspectives. This environment will not only foster your growth but also encourage vulnerability, allowing you to refine your message and build confidence as you develop your unique voice in ministry. Engaging in constructive discussions and sharing experiences with fellow preachers will empower you to embrace challenges and learn from one another, ultimately enhancing your effectiveness in delivering the truth.

Receiving feedback from different perspectives is essential for you as a young preacher. It helps refine your communication skills and allows you to connect more effectively with your congregation. Remember, each member brings unique experiences and ways of understanding the world. By actively seeking feedback, you can tailor your messages to resonate with a broader audience, ensuring that the truth you share is accessible and relatable to everyone.

Creating a safe and non-judgmental space for feedback will also encourage you to cultivate humility and a willingness to learn. When you remain open to feedback, you demonstrate a genuine desire to grow and improve as a communicator of God's truth. This humility not only deepens your understanding but also sets a positive example for your congregation, fostering a culture of continuous learning and growth.

To establish this safe environment, you need two key ingredients: trust and respect. These elements create a secure and welcoming space where honest feedback can flourish. Let's explore how you can cultivate trust and respect in your ministry.

The Importance of Trust and Respect

Trust and *respect* help foster a culture of open communication about feedback. When you establish a foundation of trust and respect, you create a safe and supportive environment where feedback can be given and received constructively. Let's explore why these elements are so important.

First, *trust* builds a sense of security and confidence between you and those offering feedback. When you trust the intentions and expertise of others, you're more likely to be open to their insights. Trust allows you to be vulnerable, knowing that the feedback you receive comes from a place of genuine care and a desire to help you grow.

Equally important, *respect* acknowledges the value and worth of everyone involved in the feedback process. When you feel respected, you're more likely to listen attentively to feedback and consider it thoughtfully. Respectful communication fosters an atmosphere where differing opinions can be shared without fear of judgment or belittlement.

In a culture of open communication, trust and respect also promote honest and transparent dialogue. When you trust that feedback is given with respect, you're more likely to be honest about your strengths and weaknesses. This honesty enables more targeted and effective feedback, leading to significant personal and professional growth.

Furthermore, trust and respect encourage collaboration and partnership. When you feel that your opinions and perspectives are valued, you're more inclined to engage in discussions and actively seek feedback from others. This collaborative approach not only strengthens your ability to handle feedback but also creates a sense of unity and shared responsibility.

In summary, cultivating trust and respect is essential for fostering a culture of open communication about feedback. By prioritizing these elements, you can embrace feedback as an opportunity for growth, enhance your preaching skills, and establish meaningful connections with those who offer wisdom.

Active Listening

If you want to receive feedback effectively, active listening is a must-have skill. It allows you to understand and appreciate the feedback provided. But first, what exactly is active listening? When handling feedback, active listening means fully engaging with the person providing the feedback. It involves giving him or her your undivided attention, maintaining an open mind, and being receptive to a new perspective. Active listening in this context includes refraining from interrupting, asking clarifying questions to ensure understanding, and acknowledging feedback without becoming defensive. By actively listening to feedback, you demonstrate respect and willingness to learn and grow and foster a constructive dialogue that could ultimately benefit you.

It is essential to actively listen to feedback, seek to understand other perspectives, and be receptive to different viewpoints. These practices enrich our personal growth and contribute to the strength of our communities.

When we actively listen to feedback, we demonstrate genuine respect and value for the opinions and experiences of others. We create an environment where individuals feel heard, acknowledged, and understood through active listening. By genuinely engaging with the feedback we receive, we can identify areas for improvement and refine our skills. Active listening allows us to build trust, foster stronger relationships, and promote effective communication within our church leadership.

Seeking to understand the perspectives of others is a powerful way to expand our thinking. Each person brings his or her unique background, experiences, and insights, which can significantly enrich our understanding of the world and the diverse needs of our congregations. By actively seeking different perspectives, we open ourselves to new ideas, challenge our biases, and foster a more inclusive and compassionate approach to leadership.

Being receptive to different viewpoints is essential to effective leadership within the church. It cultivates an environment where individuals feel safe to express their thoughts and beliefs, which helps to create a sense of belonging and empowerment. We create collaborative problem solving, innovation, and growth opportunities by embracing diverse viewpoints. It allows us to bridge divides and build bridges of understanding.

As you can see, actively listening to feedback, seeking to understand others' perspectives and being receptive to different viewpoints are important qualities for effective leadership within the church. These practices empower us to create inclusive spaces, nurture strong relationships, and foster a sense of belonging. By embodying these qualities, we can lead with compassion and wisdom, inspiring and guiding others on their spiritual journeys.

By humbling ourselves, we acknowledge that we don't have all the answers and that there's always room for improvement. It allows us to be open to different perspectives and ideas. When we approach feedback humbly, we create an environment where growth and learning can flourish. Being willing to learn means being receptive to feedback, even if it may be challenging or uncomfortable to hear. It's about recognizing feedback as an opportunity to expand our knowledge and skills. Embracing a learning mindset allows us to develop and evolve continuously.

So, young preacher, let's encourage each other to approach feedback with humility and a genuine desire to learn. Let's see it as an opportunity for growth and keep striving to become the best versions of ourselves.

Separating Feedback from Self-Worth

Imagine a preacher who is delivering a sermon to his congregation. Afterward, a congregation member approaches him with some constructive feedback. The preacher, however, takes the feedback personally and interprets it as a reflection of his self-worth.

Rather than separating the feedback from his self-worth, the preacher might feel attacked or defensive. He might internalize the feedback as a personal attack on his abilities or character, leading to feelings of inadequacy or self-doubt. This could hinder his growth as a preacher and negatively impact his relationship with the congregation.

This same preacher could have separated the feedback from his self-worth by taking advantage of the valuable opportunity for growth and improvement. Then, by remaining open to receiving constructive criticism, the preacher could have paved the way to more refined preaching skills and deep connections with his congregation.

Preachers, just like anyone else, must recognize that feedback does not reflect their worth as individuals. Feedback is an opportunity for maturation and development, and it gives them a chance to refine their skills and enhance their impact. By separating feedback from self-worth, preachers can embrace feedback with an open mind, learn from it, and continue to inspire and connect with their congregation in meaningful ways.

But when we tie our self-worth to feedback, we risk allowing the criticism—or *praise*—of others to define who we are as individuals.

Instead, we should view feedback as an opportunity. By recognizing that feedback is about our actions or behaviors, not our inherent worth, we can approach it with an open mind and a willingness to learn. When we separate feedback from personal identity, we can better distinguish between constructive criticism and personal attacks. We can objectively evaluate the feedback, apply useful insights, and do away with unfounded or irrelevant comments. This empowers us to make positive changes without compromising our sense of self.

Each one of us is unique and valuable just as we are. Embracing feedback as a roadmap that shows us where to adjust while simultaneously maintaining a solid sense of self allows us to continuously improve and evolve without losing sight of our inherent worth and identity.

So rather than internalizing criticism, let's detach it from our understanding of our value and shift our perspective. Let's view feedback as a tool for maximizing our potential. Without feedback from trusted authority figures, friends, and congregation members, we're left to our own assumptions about our level of effectiveness in the pulpit. Wouldn't it be better to *know* whether we're truly making an impact on the people we serve so we can grow and adjust accordingly? I certainly think so!

Applying Feedback

Feedback can be very positive, but its value lies in how we apply it. It's like having a treasure map—it's only valuable if we follow it and discover the hidden treasure. Likewise, merely listening to feedback will not result in growth or maturation. We must take the next step and *apply* the wisdom and advice given to us. Applying feedback requires us to take action based on the observations and suggestions of those watching us. Actively incorporating the valuable insight of others into our work or actions requires us to make necessary adjustments and strive for better outcomes.

It's never fun to hear what we may be doing wrong or where we fall short in our efforts, but without intentional action we will never become the effective ministers God has called us to be. We must be willing to set our egos aside and to be made uncomfortable in order to grow into preachers who not only speak the Word of God but do so in such a way that changes lives.

Strategies for Applying Feedback

In my experience, I've learned a few strategies that can help a young preacher effectively apply feedback.

First, as we've discussed in this chapter, be sure to receive feedback with an open mind and a teachable spirit. This mindset allows you to be receptive to different perspectives and ideas. Next, take the time to reflect on the feedback received. Consider the points raised and how they align with your goals or objectives. This reflection helps clarify which areas can be improved. Once you have reflected, create an action plan. Break down the feedback into actionable steps and set specific goals for improvement. This way, you can systematically work toward implementing the suggested changes.

Another effective strategy is to seek clarification if needed. Feel free to ask for more information if you need further guidance or understanding. Clearing up any uncertainties will ensure that you appropriately apply the insights you received.

Lastly, track your progress and evaluate the impact of the changes you have made. It is important to regularly assess how the applied feedback has influenced your work or actions. This ongoing evaluation allows for continuous improvement and adjustment as needed.

Imagine you've recently delivered a sermon and received feedback from a congregation member that your delivery style could improve. Instead of getting discouraged, you decide to embrace the feedback and work on enhancing your preaching skills. As you reflect on the observations made by the congregation member, you remember your tone, pacing, and body language during your most recent sermon delivery and consider the feedback in light of your goals and aspirations as a preacher.

Next, you create an action plan to address the feedback. You decide to practice your delivery in front of a mirror and record yourself to analyze your speaking style. You also seek out resources like books and online courses on public speaking or preaching techniques to learn new ways to improve.

As you apply these strategies, you actively listen to yourself and to others. You pay attention to the feedback you receive from trusted mentors or congregation members and adjust your delivery accordingly.

Over time, with practice and dedication, you begin to notice improvements in your preaching style, and your delivery becomes more engaging, confident, and impactful. The congregation responds positively, and you feel a deeper connection with your audience.

Although this was just an imaginative exercise, you'll find that by regularly applying these principles in your life, you will mature into an effective minister of the Gospel who consistently makes a lasting impact on those who encounter you. Although the gift God gave you is perfect, it has to flow through you, an imperfect vessel. Therefore, it is your responsibility to do everything within your power to become the best version of yourself so the gift of God can flow freely and effectively.

Cultivating a Feedback Culture

Preaching communities should indeed be safe places that foster a feedback culture. Creating an environment where feedback is valued and respected allows for growth, learning, and improvement among preachers, young and old alike. In a safe preaching community, individuals feel comfortable sharing their thoughts, ideas, and concerns without fear of judgment or reprisal. This open and supportive atmosphere encourages honest feedback, which can be constructive and uplifting. It allows preachers to receive input on their sermons, delivery style, and overall impact, helping them refine their skills and connect more deeply with their congregation.

A feedback culture in preaching communities promotes collaboration and mutual respect. It encourages active listening, empathy, and understanding among all members. By cultivating a safe space for feedback, preaching communities can create an environment where everyone feels heard, valued, and empowered. It strengthens the bond between preachers, giving a sense of shared purpose.

It's important to remember that a feedback culture doesn't just magically appear. Cultivating a culture where feedback is valued and embraced takes intentional effort and nurturing.

Here are some ways to actively cultivate a feedback culture:

1. **Make It a Safe Space:** Create an environment where everyone feels supported and safe to share their thoughts and ideas without judgment.
2. **Lead by Example**: Show that being open and vulnerable is okay. Share your challenges and mistakes; let them know it's all part of the learning process.
3. **Listen Up**: Teach the importance of active listening. Encourage them to pay attention and understand what others say before responding.
4. **Give Helpful Feedback**: Focus on specific things someone can improve rather than criticizing anyone personally. Offer suggestions for how someone can get better and also highlight strengths.
5. **Create Feedback Opportunities**: Set up ways to give and receive feedback, like feedback sessions or anonymous surveys. This makes it easier for people to share their thoughts and ideas.
6. **Embrace Growth**: Help others see feedback as a chance to grow and improve rather than something negative. Encourage people to adopt a positive mindset and see feedback as a valuable tool that is necessary for development.
7. **Celebrate Wins**: When others apply feedback and make positive changes, celebrate their successes. This shows that their efforts are recognized and encourages growth.

Ultimately, a culture of feedback is beneficial for anyone willing to learn and grow. But what happens when you receive conflicting input from multiple sources? How do we accept and apply opposite insights? It's important to remember that not all feedback will align perfectly, and it's not your responsibility to please everyone who provides feedback—particularly when it comes from congregation members.

When you encounter conflicting feedback, take time to prayerfully consider the source and substance of each piece of advice. Ask yourself:

- Is the feedback grounded in biblical truth?
- Does it align with my calling and the message God has placed on my heart?
- Will applying this feedback strengthen my connection with the congregation or dilute the truth I'm endeavoring to communicate?

Weigh each perspective with discernment and seek to understand the heart behind the feedback without feeling pressured to act on every suggestion. It's also wise to seek counsel from trusted mentors or peers in ministry who can offer objective advice and help you determine which feedback will most benefit your growth.

Young preacher, always approach feedback with a growth mindset. You should see it as an opportunity for growth and improvement rather than a personal attack. Embrace the idea that constructive criticism is not a reflection of your worth but a chance to refine your skills and become even better at what you do. But, ultimately, your responsibility is not to please everyone who offers an opinion. Your mandate is to faithfully steward the message God has entrusted to you. Learning to balance humility with discernment ensures you remain open to growth while staying true to the call on your life.

— 99 —

FEEDBACK

IS A VALUABLE RESOURCE FOR *growth* AND DEVELOPMENT. EMBRACE IT WITH AN OPEN MIND AND A LOVE FOR KNOWLEDGE, AND YOU'LL CONTINUE TO GROW AS A PREACHER.

— 99 —

Chapter 9

Balancing Ministry and Personal Life

Did you know that studies have shown that maintaining a healthy work-life balance improves overall well-being and enhances productivity and effectiveness in ministry? It's fascinating how finding that equilibrium between serving others and caring for ourselves can benefit both areas of our lives. It's a reminder that investing in our well-being is not selfish but a way to enhance our ability to serve others in ministry.

When we serve others, we can positively impact people's lives, bring hope, and show God's love in practical ways that can be seen and felt at the heart level. It allows us to be a blessing to those around us and contribute to the well-being of our communities. That is the way we fulfill our call. When we use our unique gifts and talents to glorify God, we make a difference in the lives of others.

Ministry has a powerful impact on individuals and communities. On an individual level, it provides guidance, support, and spiritual nourishment, helping people deepen their faith, find healing, and grow personally. Through ministry, individuals discover their purpose, develop their gifts, and strengthen their relationship with God.

On a community level, ministry fosters unity, compassion, and social transformation. It brings people together, creating a sense of belonging and connection. Ministry initiatives like outreach programs and community service address social issues, eliminate suffering, and promote positive change. By serving the community, ministry inspires hope, brings reconciliation, and contributes to society's overall well-being. The impact of ministry is far-reaching, touching lives and making a lasting difference.

But self-care, meaningful relationships, and personal well-being are also fundamental aspects of our lives. Taking care of ourselves allows us to recharge, maintain a healthy balance, and be at our best to serve others. It's like putting on our own oxygen mask before helping others on a plane. When prioritizing self-care, we have more energy, clarity, and resilience to pour into our ministry and relationships.

Making our personal lives a priority positively impacts our effectiveness in ministry. A healthy personal life allows us to bring our best selves to our ministry work. When we care for our physical, mental, and emotional health, we have everything we need to serve others. By investing in self-care, we can avoid burnout and maintain a healthy work-life balance. This enables us to be more present and engaged in our ministry, providing better support and guidance to those we serve. Additionally, when we prioritize our personal growth and development, we continuously learn and acquire new skills to enhance our ministry's effectiveness.

It's all about balance. When we prioritize our personal life *alongside* our ministry, we create a healthy rhythm that allows us to recharge. Taking time for ourselves, engaging in activities we enjoy, and nurturing relationships outside of ministry all contribute to our overall well-being. This, in turn, enhances our effectiveness and longevity in our ministry work. Finding that balance can be challenging, but it's worth the effort.

Neglecting our personal lives can hinder our effectiveness in ministry. When we pour all our time and energy solely into ministry, we risk burning out and experiencing fatigue. Taking care of our personal lives allows us to recharge and bring fresh perspectives and energy to our ministry work. So finding that balance is critical, young preacher.

Because of that, in this chapter, we'll explore practical strategies and insights for achieving a healthy balance between ministry and personal life. Let's explore the necessary tools for a fulfilling and sustainable journey.

Defining Ministry and Personal Life

To me, ministry is about serving others and fulfilling our calling to positively impact the lives of those around us. It's about sharing love, compassion, and support with others, whether it's through teaching, mentoring, or any other form of service. Ministry holds great significance in my life because it allows me to contribute to something greater than myself and to be a source of encouragement and inspiration to others. It brings me joy and fulfillment to make a difference in the lives of those I serve.

Defining what ministry means to you is super important. Once you clearly understand what it is, you can truly appreciate its significance and hold it in the proper regard.

There are several aspects to consider when it comes to ministry. First, there's the aspect of service, where we actively engage in helping and supporting others. Then, there's the aspect of leadership, where we guide and inspire those around us. Additionally, ministry involves spreading love and compassion and sharing the message of faith. It also includes teaching, mentoring, and being a source of encouragement. These different aspects all come together to create a well-rounded and impactful ministry.

Personal life is also about finding a balance between work or ministry and taking care of ourselves. A critical aspect of personal life is nurturing relationships. This means investing time and effort into building and maintaining meaningful connections with family, friends, and loved ones. This becomes your "circle of life" that you can run to for strength and encouragement.

As a preacher, having a supportive circle of people who understand and handle your weaknesses with compassion and honesty is non-negotiable. Having a trusted group of friends, mentors, or fellow preachers can provide you with the support and encouragement you need to stay on course and finish strong. They can offer guidance, a listening ear, and help you navigate any challenges or vulnerabilities you may face. Remember, we all have our weaknesses, and having a circle that understands and supports you will make a world of difference in your journey as a preacher.

Let's look at Jesus as an example. When He was going through a challenging time in the garden of Gethsemane, out of the twelve individuals He discipled, He chose to have only three individuals accompany Him. It shows the importance of having a small, trusted group of people during moments of struggle. Jesus understood the value of having a close-knit circle that could provide support, encouragement, and understanding during difficult times. It's a powerful reminder to build those relationships and surround ourselves with a few trusted individuals who can journey with us.

Another aspect of personal life is practicing self-care. This involves prioritizing our physical, mental, and emotional well-being. It's about taking time to rest, recharge, and engage in activities that bring us joy and fulfillment. Whether it's going for a walk, reading a book, or indulging in a hobby, self-care helps us rejuvenate and maintain a healthy balance.

So when it comes to taking care of ourselves, everyone's got their way of doing it. I've found that therapy, hitting the gym, and going on cruises really do the trick for me. These things are totally different from each other, but they all help me recharge and feel refreshed. It's like giving myself a boost in other areas of my life. Find what works for you!

Lastly, personal life also includes pursuing personal growth. This means continuously learning, exploring new interests, and setting goals for ourselves.

It's about embracing opportunities for self-improvement and challenging ourselves to reach our full potential. Whether taking a new course, learning a musical instrument, or acquiring new skills, personal growth keeps us engaged, motivated, and excited about life outside of work and ministry.

Find that sweet spot where you can thrive in all areas of your life. Remember, it's essential to prioritize your personal life alongside your work or ministry to lead a fulfilling and balanced life. Caring for your mind, body, and spirit is important, especially for young preachers. Start now so you don't burn out later. Finding what works for you and incorporating it into your routine can make all the difference in the world.

The Challenges

Balancing ministry and personal life can be quite a juggling act, but it's a challenge that many of us face. As preachers, we're passionate about our calling, and we are dedicated to serving others. However, we must remember that caring for ourselves and nurturing our personal lives is just as important. Let's take some time to discuss common challenges when trying to maintain this delicate balance.

One challenge that is commonly faced is the demand for our

time and energy. If we're not careful, ministry can be all-consuming, with endless responsibilities, meetings, and events. It's easy to get caught up in the whirlwind and neglect our personal lives. We may find ourselves constantly on the go, feeling like there needs to be more time for ourselves or our loved ones. This can lead to burnout and strain in our relationships.

Another common challenge is setting boundaries. As ministers, we have a heart for helping others, and it's natural to want to be available at all times. However, this can result in our personal lives taking a backseat. We may struggle to say no or feel guilty when prioritizing our needs. But establishing healthy boundaries and communicating our limitations is required in order to avoid becoming overwhelmed.

Finding time for self-care is another challenge. We pour so much of ourselves into ministry that we may neglect our own well-being. Our spiritual, physical, and emotional health can suffer if we don't carve out time for rest, relaxation, and rejuvenation. It's essential to prioritize self-care activities that recharge us.

Maintaining healthy relationships can also be a challenge. Our dedication to ministry can sometimes strain our relationships with family and friends. We may miss important events, neglect quality time, or need help with being fully present with our loved ones. We must invest in our relationships, communicate openly, and make intentional efforts to create a healthy balance.

Navigating the expectations of others can also be challenging. People may have certain expectations of us as ministers, and meeting everyone's needs and desires can be difficult. We may feel pulled in different directions, trying to please everyone, all the while neglecting our own well-being. Young preacher, please understand that you can't do it all; it's okay to prioritize your needs from time to time and make choices that align with your values and calling.

In the midst of these challenges, it's important to remember that finding balance is a continuous journey. It requires self-awareness, intentional decision-making, and regular reflection. It also calls for grace and flexibility. We need to be kind to ourselves when we stumble or feel overwhelmed. It's okay to ask for help and seek support. Remember, you're not alone in this journey.

Your calling goes beyond just preaching; it's about living out what you believe every single day. Ministry isn't just about what happens on Sunday mornings—it's also about how you show up in your personal life.

Navigating this journey can be tricky. You'll have to juggle things like living a holy life, handling money wisely, making time for prayer (not just for sermon prep), and balancing your ministry with your family. Each of these areas impacts not only your effectiveness as a preacher but also how you are perceived as a leader.

Think of these topics as the building blocks that uphold your ministry. They're there help you live out your calling while still taking care of the other important things in life. So, let's dive into these key areas and see how you can keep everything in sync.

Pursuing Holiness and Righteous Living

As a young preacher, your lifestyle speaks just as loudly as your sermons. People are watching even when you're unaware, and they take their cues from you about what's right, what's acceptable, and what's expected of a follower of Christ. While we all face struggles, it's crucial to actively pursue righteous living. This doesn't mean you have to be perfect, but it does mean striving to live a life that reflects God's holiness.

Righteous living isn't about appearances; it's about integrity. What you do in private matters just as much as what you do in public. Integrity demands consistency between your words and your actions, and it's this integrity that builds trust with your congregation. Set a standard not just with your preaching, but with your life. People need to see in you an example of someone who is genuinely walking with God.

Ask yourself:
• Are my actions aligned with my preaching?
• Am I modeling the kind of life I encourage others to live?

Handling Money With Integrity

Money can be a delicate topic in ministry, but it's one that cannot be avoided. Whether you're preaching about finances, handling church money, or receiving honorariums for speaking engagements, how you handle money speaks to your character.

When discussing money from the pulpit, make sure you're grounded in biblical principles of stewardship and generosity. Avoid manipulation or pressure when addressing financial matters. Similarly, in your personal life, it's important to handle finances with integrity. Be transparent, be accountable, and remember that your actions in this area reflect not just on you, but on the church and, ultimately, on God.

Key Considerations:
- Does the way you approach money align with your integrity and calling?
- Are you transparent and ethical in handling both personal and church finances?

Prayer and Study for Personal Growth

It's easy to fall into the trap of only praying and studying when preparing sermons. However, it's essential to your spiritual well-being to have a vibrant personal relationship with God beyond sermon preparation. Preaching regularly doesn't replace your need for personal prayer and study. It's through personal time with God that your soul is nourished, your spirit is strengthened, and your ministry is sustained.

As a young preacher, make time to feed yourself spiritually. Your congregation will benefit from your growth, but more importantly, your personal relationship with God will thrive.

Practical Tips:
1. Set aside dedicated time each week for personal prayer and Bible study that is not related to sermon preparation.
2. Engage with devotional materials, theological works, or Bible studies to deepen your understanding of Scripture.
3. Guard and cherish your time with God and regard it as the foundation of your ministry.

Balancing Ministry and Family

One of the biggest challenges you'll face as a young preacher is balancing your ministry with your family life. Both are important, but sometimes they will seem to compete for your attention. How do you choose when to prioritize ministry over family, or family over ministry?

The key is recognizing that both are callings from God. You're called to serve in ministry, but you're also called to serve your family. Healthy boundaries are crucial. There will be times when ministry needs your immediate attention, but there will also be times when your family must come first.

Ask Yourself:

- Am I sacrificing my family for ministry, or am I sacrificing ministry for my family?
- How can I establish boundaries that protect both my family and my ministry?

Strategies and Practical Tips

Finding a balance between ministry and personal life can indeed be challenging. It requires intentional effort and constant adjustments. However, the good news is that it is a skill that can be developed over time. You can gradually find a rhythm that works for you by implementing practical strategies. Remember, it's a journey, and making mistakes along the way is okay. Embrace the process of growth and learning, and you'll find that balance becoming more attainable. Here are some practical tips and strategies to help you navigate this balance:

1. **Take Care of Yourself**: It's super important to make time for things that make you feel good physically, emotionally, and spiritually. Do activities that recharge you, like exercising, pursuing hobbies, praying, or spending time in nature.
2. **Set Boundaries**: Create clear boundaries between your ministry and personal life. Let people know when you're available or when you need some "me" time. Don't be afraid to say no, and ask for help when needed.
3. **Make a Schedule**: Plan out your time so you have a good

balance between ministry, personal affairs, and rest. Stick to it, but be flexible when unexpected things come up.

4. **Listen Up**: When you talk to people, really listen. Show them you care and understand what they're going through. It builds better relationships.

5. **Talk It Out**: Encourage open and honest communication with your team and loved ones. Create a safe space for everyone to share their thoughts and needs.

6. **Take Breaks**: Give yourself regular breaks and vacations. You need time to relax, recharge, and spend time with loved ones.

7. **Find Support**: Surround yourself with people who understand your challenges and can offer guidance and encouragement. They'll keep you on track.

8. **Reflect**: Take time to think about how things are going in your ministry and personal life and make adjustments as needed.

Finding balance in life is a journey that requires patience and consistency. By implementing these tips, you'll gradually create a more fulfilling and balanced life. It won't happen overnight, but you'll see positive changes with time and practice. Achieving a healthy balance with these strategies and tips can tremendously impact your ministry and overall well-being. It allows you to serve others with renewed energy and passion while taking care of yourself. When you find that balance, you can meaningfully invest in your ministry, making a impact on the lives of others. At the same time, you can nurture your personal relationships, pursue your interests, and recharge your spirit. It's a beautiful mix that brings fulfillment, joy, and longevity to your ministry and personal life.

Unplug To Plug In

It's pretty common to hear people say they need to "unplug" when they're feeling overwhelmed or burnt out from their work. It's as if they're craving an escape from the demands and pressures of their current responsibilities.

Taking time to unplug can be a healthy way to recharge and find balance in our lives. However, our time has created a culture that when we need to unplug, we often stop there without considering what we can plug into to build ourselves up. And Jesus set a powerful example for us in this regard.

In the gospels, we see Jesus frequently leaving the crowds to commune with the Father. He sought solitude and quietness away from the demands and distractions of the world. In these moments of unplugging, Jesus intentionally plugged into God, nurturing his relationship with the Father and drawing strength and guidance from Him.

By following Jesus' example, we can understand the importance of unplugging from the noise and busyness of life to intentionally plug into God. Just as Jesus sought communion with the Father, we too can seek moments of solitude and stillness to connect with God through prayer, meditation, worship, and reflection on His Word. In these moments, we can find spiritual nourishment, guidance, and renewal.

When we unplug from the world and plug into God, we open ourselves to His presence, wisdom, and transformative power. Through this connection, we can find true rest, peace, and fulfillment. As we prioritize our relationship with God and seek His guidance, we become better equipped to navigate life's challenges and fulfill our purpose.

Unplugging from the busyness of life to plug into God is a powerful way to find balance in both ministry and personal life. When we intentionally set aside time to connect with God, it rejuvenates our spirits, strengthens our faith, and provides us with the guidance and wisdom we need to navigate the various aspects of our lives.

In the midst of our busy schedules and responsibilities, it's easy to get caught up in the demands of ministry and personal obligations. However, when we prioritize spending time with God, we tap into a source of peace, strength, and clarity that enables us to approach our roles and relationships with renewed purpose and perspective.

By unplugging from the distractions and noise of the world, we create space for intimate moments with God. In these moments of connection, we find solace, receive guidance, and experience a deep sense of fulfillment.

Prioritizing our relationship with God naturally influences how we approach ministry and personal life. We gain a greater understanding of our calling, discernment in decision-making, and a heart of compassion and service toward others. We become more attuned to God's leading, which helps us navigate the demands and challenges of ministry while also nurturing our relationships and well-being.

Remember the importance of plugging into God as you seek to balance ministry and personal life. Prioritize that connection time and allow it to shape and guide every aspect of your life. By grounding yourself in your faith and seeking God's presence, you'll find a sense of purpose and fulfillment that will empower you to thrive in ministry and personal endeavors.

So, young preacher, if you don't remember anything else we have discussed in this final chapter, remember the importance of unplugging to plug into God. Follow Jesus' example and seek moments of solitude and communion with the Father. In doing so, you will find the strength, guidance, and fulfillment that comes from being connected to the source of all life. Keep seeking that balance, and know that God is with you every step of the way!

— 99 —

WHEN WE UNPLUG FROM THE WORLD AND PLUG INTO GOD, WE OPEN OURSELVES TO HIS PRESENCE, WISDOM, AND TRANSFORMATIVE *power.*

— 99 —

Final Word of Encouragement

Hey there, young preacher! Congratulations on completing your manual—it's a remarkable achievement! I'm thrilled to have the opportunity to share some words of encouragement with you as you embark on this incredible journey.

First and foremost, I want to affirm your dedication and passion for preaching. Your desire to share the message of God's love and truth is truly inspiring. Your voice matters, and your unique perspective has the power to touch hearts and transform lives.

As you enter this calling, remember that growth and development are essential. Embrace the challenge of continuous learning and improvement. Seek out mentors, attend workshops, and dive into the rich resources available to you. Allow yourself to be stretched and refined; through these experiences, you will blossom into an even more impactful preacher.

But growth isn't just about honing your speaking skills; it's also about cultivating your character. As you stand before others, remember to lead by example. Let your actions align with your words, and strive to embody the love, compassion, and humility of Jesus Christ. People are looking for powerful sermons and authentic lives that reflect the message being preached.

Don't be afraid to take risks and step out of your comfort zone. The path of a preacher can be challenging, but it is filled with incredible rewards. Embrace the challenges that come your way, for they will shape you into a resilient and empathetic servant of God. Remember that you are not alone, even in moments of doubt or discouragement. Lean on your faith, seek support from your fellow preachers, and trust in the guidance of the Holy Spirit.

Lastly, always keep sight of the profound impact you can have on the lives of others. Your words have the power to heal, inspire, and ignite transformation. Whether speaking to a small congregation or a vast audience, remember that each person you reach is a precious soul. Approach your preaching with a heart full of love, grace, and a genuine desire to see lives transformed by the power of God's Word.

So, my dear young preacher, may you be encouraged to continue growing, developing, and stepping into the fullness of your calling as you venture forth. Embrace the challenges, nurture your character, and let your light shine brightly. The world needs your voice, passion, and unwavering commitment to share the Good News. Keep shining, keep growing, and keep making a difference!

—*Caleb R. Edge*

-CALEB R. EDGE

ABOUT THE AUTHOR

Caleb R. Edge, the senior pastor of The Restoration Church, is a dynamic preacher and mentor who has been impacting lives from a young age. With a passion for spreading God's Word, Caleb began his preaching journey at the remarkable age of 13. Since then, he has continued to inspire and empower others through his ministry.

As the senior pastor of The Restoration Church, Caleb leads a vibrant and growing congregation in two locations: Americus, GA, and Cordele, GA. His dedication to serving his community and guiding others in their faith journey has made him a respected figure in the church.

Beyond his local ministry, Caleb has also had the privilege of traveling and engaging in itinerant ministry, sharing his powerful message with diverse audiences. His experiences on the road have allowed him to connect with people from all walks of life and witness the transformative power of God's love.

In addition to his preaching endeavors, Caleb has mentored and counseled numerous young preachers. His guidance and wisdom have helped shape the next generation of preachers, equipping them with the tools they need to navigate the challenges and joys of ministry.

Through his writing, Caleb aims to inspire and encourage others to embrace their calling, live out their faith, and positively impact the world. His passion for mentoring and his experiences in ministry make his words resonate with authenticity and wisdom.

CALEBEDGE.COM

@CALEB.EDGE

@CALEBREDGE

www.ingramcontent.com/pod-product-compliance
Lightning Source LLC
Chambersburg PA
CBHW051633120626
46551CB00014B/2063